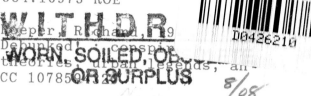

DEBUNKED!

DEBUNKED!

CONSPIRACY THEORIES, URBAN LEGENDS, AND EVIL PLOTS OF THE 21ST CENTURY

RICHARD ROEPER

CHICAGO
REVIEW
PRESS

Library of Congress Cataloging-in-Publication Data

Roeper, Richard, 1959–
  Debunked! : conspiracy theories, urban legends, and evil plots of the
21st century / Richard Roeper. — 1st ed.
      p. cm.
  Includes index.
  ISBN 978-1-55652-707-4
  1. Conspiracies—United States. 2. Urban folklore—United States. 3.
Conspiracies. 4. Urban folklore. I. Title.

  E169.Z83R63 2008
  364.10973—dc22

                                          2008001541

Cover design: Joan Sommers Design
Interior design: Jonathan Hahn

Published by Chicago Review Press, Incorporated
814 North Franklin Street
Chicago, Illinois 60610
ISBN 978-1-55652-707-4
Printed in the United States of America
5 4 3 2 1

CONTENTS

Introduction vii

I EVIL PLOTS

1 The Steel Didn't Have to Melt 3
2 The Clinton Kill Count 19
3 The Conspiracy That Won't Di 23
4 The Kennedy Assassination, 1999 Edition 29

II THE MEDIA

5 It's a Media Blackout 39
6 Katrina and the Waves of Misinformation 47
7 The Vast Left-Wing Conspiracy 55

III SPORTS AND GAMING

8 Online Poker Conspiracies Flushed Out 59
9 The NFL: National Fixed-Ball League 67
10 Casino Culture 83
11 Curt Schilling and the Bloody Red Sox 91

IV ENTERTAINMENT

12 The Sopranos' Last Supper 99
13 The Secret of *The Secret* 105
14 Beware of False *Idol* Votes 117

V **BUSINESS**

15 I'll Have an Iced Grande Vanilla Nonfat Conspiracy 127
16 Rummy and the Bird Flu 135
17 *Evian* is *Naive* Spelled Backwards 139

VI **MIRACLES**

18 Dead Man Talking! 145
19 It's a Miracle—That Some People Believe This Stuff 153

VII **THE CULTURE**

20 The "War" on Christmas 165
21 Classical Gas 177
22 Warning: Jager Bombs Can Kill You! 181
23 The Godless Dollar Coin 187
24 Rock Me Nostradamus 191

VIII **POLITICS**

25 Bush's Mystery Bulge 197
26 Barack Obama: Radical Muslim! 203
27 The Hate Crime Prevention Act 209

IX **MOVIES**

28 Of *Soylent Green* and *Men in Black*: The Best and
Worst Conspiracy Movies Ever Made 215

Index 237

INTRODUCTION

Paraphrasing George Bernard Shaw, Robert F. Kennedy famously said, "Some men see things the way they are, and ask 'Why?' I dream of things that never were, and ask 'Why not?'"

Paraphrasing myself (an act of self-involvement that is still legal in 38 states): Some people look at things the way they are and express a healthy skepticism while keeping an open mind and listening to hard evidence and common sense.

And some people look at things the way they are—from man walking on the moon to the Super Bowl to the events of 9/11—and say, "IT'S ALL A LIE!!!!!"

Those people are conspiracy theorists.

In my 20 years as a journalist, I'd like to think I've developed a cynical shell and honed my bullshit detector. My first response to any outrageous story is to say, "OK, wait a minute; let's make sure we have this right before we go any further."

As the slogan of the famous Chicago City News Bureau advised, "If your mother says she loves you, check it out."

We don't take things at face value in my business.

If an athlete or a politician says he's retiring to "spend more time with the family," we roll our eyes and compare notes on the real reasons for his exit.

If someone disappears and the spouse appears at the press conference sobbing and pleading for information and begging for the "kidnappers" to contact him, we look at the spouse as the first "person of interest" in the case.

When a candidate who says he's an "outsider" raises a record amount of funds, we look into his political connections. If corruption rears its head, we follow the money.

If somebody calls the city desk and says, "I just saw Bigfoot at the 7-Eleven buying a burrito!" we laugh. (But we take her number just in case.)

And when something smells of conspiracy or cover-up, we dive in headfirst in an effort to uncover the plot.

I don't believe for a second that we live in a conspiracy-free world. Ever since I was 14 and I saw the president of the United States announce his resignation on live television, I have understood there's often a much more complicated story behind the story. A "third-rate burglary" in a hotel can lead to so much more.

Of course some business executives sometimes conspire to cheat their employees and realize huge profits. Of course some government leaders sometimes conspire to mislead their constituents. Of course some individuals and groups act in collusion to commit crimes.

And you know what? We know about these things because the conspiracies are eventually *uncovered*. Somebody talks, or something leaks, or some trail of evidence is uncovered—and the jig is up.

It's not as if those guys from Enron are laughing it up on the beach right now.

It's easy to understand how folklore, rumors, and conspiracy theories flourished in supposedly less sophisticated times. As recently as a generation ago, such stories were spread largely by word of mouth or via old-fashioned communication methods such as pamphlets and chain letters. It took even longer to debunk the lies.

Ah, but in the 21st century, the concept of the global village has become reality. Thanks to the Internet, anyone with access to a computer can tap into a wealth of resources that dwarf the largest libraries. So how can folklore, rumors, tall tales, myths, and conspiracy theories thrive in a world where the truth is at everyone's fingertips?

Problem is, the half-truths, innuendos, speculative claims, and outright falsehoods have also grown over the Internet, like the ivy covering the outfield walls of Wrigley Field. Instead of being relegated to a corner marked "Kooks and Crackpots," the conspiracy theorists stand side by side with legitimate news sources and fact-based findings. On the cool, flat, colorful computer screen, a well-designed conspiracy Web site looks just as legitimate as the site of the *New York Times* or CNN.

Instead of weakening the B.S. movement, the information and misinformation explosion gave it more strength. If you advanced a conspiracy theory in the 1980s, it might catch a ride on the word-of-mouth express, or it might just die. If you put forward a conspiracy theory in the 21st century, it'll live on the Internet *forever*.

One of the most incredible things about all the big-time conspiracy theories percolating on the Internet is that the so-called conspiracies remain secret, even with so many people asking so many questions about so many allegedly suspicious activities.

Nobody involved in, say, the assassination of John F. Kennedy, or the fake moon landing, or the attacks of 9/11, ever breaks ranks and produces a smoking gun. Hundreds if not thousands of people would have to be in on these world-shattering conspiracies—yet there's never any hard proof of such plots. You'd think some disgruntled conspirator would rat out his bosses, or some member of an evil cabal would experience a crisis of conscience and come clean, or some enterprising journalist would dig up some hard evidence of one of these conspiracies—enough to blow the whole thing up.

But it doesn't happen, because it can't happen, because the conspiracies aren't real.

Over the closing credits of the 2007 documentary *In the Shadow of the Moon*, many of the Apollo astronauts who journeyed to the moon laugh at the notion of a conspiracy. One Apollo veteran notes that if two people have a secret, it usually gets out; how were thousands persuaded to keep quiet? Another says, "If we faked [flights to the moon], why did we do it *nine times?*"

This is a messy, chaotic, sometimes cruel world, where lone assassins can bring down great leaders and planes can explode in the sky because of technical malfunctions—and 19 murderous hijackers can forever change the world on one morning in September.

When I watch an NFL playoff game and there appears to be a bad call, I assume the referee made a mistake, as all human beings do from time to time. When a conspiracy buff sees the same play, he throws his hands up and mutters, "They got to the refs."

He doesn't say this in a half-joking tone, nor does he pose it as a question—"I wonder if they got to the refs?" As sure as the Chicago Bears' colors are navy and orange, the paranoid fan is absolutely positive the official was paid off to "throw" the game. And some of the players are probably in on it as well!

Ask the conspiracy theorist for proof of such a claim, and he will become irritated with you—exasperated at your naivete. He doesn't have any *evidence*, but come on, "everyone" knows pro football and basketball games are fixed so that the playoffs will run for as long as possible and the major-market teams will make the finals.

The believers in these myths and legends and conspiracies often say, "Prove me wrong," because that's a lot easier to say than "I haven't got the first shred of evidence to prove I'm right."

Conspiracy theorists love the *argumentum ad ignorantiam*—the "argument from ignorance," which is the practice of arguing that a theory or belief is true simply because it has not been proved false beyond any shadow of a whisper of a doubt.

Many theories about 9/11 begin with "You'll never convince me" or "I don't see how" or "There's no way . . ."

You'll never convince me 19 mopes with box cutters commandeered four planes.

I don't see how the World Trade Center collapsed from the impact of those two planes.

There's no way a Boeing 757 could have hit the Pentagon without making a bigger hole.

For the conspiracy theorist, a lack of understanding of an event or an unwillingness to accept substantial evidence somehow constitutes "proof" that *his* version of events is more plausible—even though the conspiracy theory is almost always far more complex and implausible than the actual chain of events.

Which is more believable: that United Airlines Flight 93 crash-landed in Pennsylvania or that Flight 93 secretly landed in Cleveland, where the passengers were whisked off to a NASA facility?

Whether we're talking about tragic news events such as Katrina and 9/11 or happy diversions such as the Super Bowl or *American Idol*, one can always find some loose threads, some inconsistencies, some unanswered questions. Most people understand that this doesn't mean there's something awry—it simply means the world is an imperfect place and our experiences are shaded in tones of gray, not black and white.

The conspiracy theorist grabs a factoid here, an erroneous news report there, sprinkles in some anecdotal evidence, throws in a few half-baked theories, stirs them all together—and presto! It's a conspiracy cocktail. Have a taste!

Just don't swallow it.

Much of this book focuses on subjects that fit the traditional definition of the conspiracy theory, for example, the voting is rigged on *American Idol* or the media are coconspirators in the secular progressive "war" on Christmas. Too many people who should know better fall for this nonsense.

We're also going to take a look at some other trends, stories, and phenomena that have captivated and conned a jarringly large percentage of the American public. From psychics talking to the dead to the Virgin Mary appearing on a grilled cheese sandwich to the utter nonsense that is *The Secret*, it is my intention to mock, lampoon, and debunk these so-called phenomena.

Whether we're talking about conspiracies, urban legends, hoaxes, scams, cons, psychic phenomena, or miracles, there's only one sensible approach to any of this stuff.

A giant glass of skepticism.

I

EVIL PLOTS

1

THE STEEL DIDN'T
HAVE TO MELT

Well your a moron Dick I will never buy or read the Sun Times after your column on Rosie today! She has more courage than you will have in your next 100 lives combined. I'm a Navy veteran and . . . I can tell you for a FACT that 9–11 was a complete and total INSIDE JOB! Keep selling your country down the river for your newspaper paycheck you are now and always will be a piece of shit traitor. You don't have the guts to print an honest 9–11 piece.

—One of the more reasoned e-mails I received from 9/11 conspiracy theorists after I wrote a column expressing doubts about Rosie O'Donnell's 9/11 opinions

If there were one point I'd like to drive into the mindsets of all the conspiracy theorists that look at the events of 9/11 not as one of the most tragic days in American history but as the mother lode of all conspiracies, it would be this:

The steel didn't have to melt.

Every time I make even a passing reference to 9/11 conspiracies on TV or radio or in my newspaper column, I hear from the indefatigable legions of 9/11 skeptics.

They send me 2,000-word rants about the "Phantom Plane" and the Pentagon.

They provide handy links to all sorts of Web sites offering "proof" of a wide-ranging 9/11 conspiracy that begins and ends with the White House.

They make claims about "secret government facilities" that house the passengers and the crews from the flights that "supposedly crashed."

They ask unanswerable questions, as if doing so somehow adds weight to their arguments.

And they inevitably trot out the supposedly irrefutable proof that preplanted explosives felled the World Trade Center. This proof hinges on the theory that jet fuel doesn't burn at a high enough temperature to melt steel, and therefore the steel didn't melt, and therefore something else had to make the buildings collapse. Something like preplanted explosive devices.

But here's the thing:

The steel didn't have to melt.

When jet fuel burns, it reaches temperatures of up to 1,500 degrees Fahrenheit, and it's true that steel won't yet melt at that temperature—but try to find an experienced firefighter who has *ever* come across fully melted steel at even the worst fire scene. (Charred and bent and distorted, yes. Melted? No.) For the towers to collapse (say it with me now), the steel frames of the WTC didn't have to melt—they had to sag and crack and experience stress, which is surely what happened. At 1,500 degrees, the steel frames would have lost 75 percent or more of their strength—and that's enough for a building to collapse.

Pointing out that jet fuel doesn't burn at temperatures high enough to melt steel has about as much relevance as pointing out it was a sunny and beautiful day in New York City on September 11, 2001.

You'd think conspiracy theorists would embrace the known facts of 9/11. After all, it *was* a conspiracy—a complicated, audacious, obscenely horrible conspiracy involving a multitude of murderous thugs acting in concert at the behest of an evil, United States–hating terrorist.

Like any such plot in recorded history, it was a messy and mistake-riddled conspiracy that could have fallen apart at any number of junctures. There is no such thing as a "perfect" conspiracy. If there were, the conspiracy theorists wouldn't know about it, because then it wouldn't be perfect, would it?

But just because it was sloppy and preventable doesn't mean it didn't happen—nor does it mean there "has" to be a more elaborate and even more devious plot behind the plot.

Before sunset on 9/11, conspiracy theorists were already working themselves into frenzied speculation about what was *really* going on. By now the 9/11 conspiracy game is an industry unto itself, with dozens of Web sites, DVDs, and books dedicated to "exposing" the "real truth" about what happened on that terrible day and who was "really" behind it.

Yet in nearly seven years, none of these hundreds of self-appointed detectives has come even close to scoring a major scoop about 9/11.

Still, they try. As if it's not mind-boggling enough to believe that planes smashed into the WTC and the Pentagon and that a fourth plane was crash-landed before it could reach Washington, D.C., and that these acts of war were carried about by murderous, suicidal maniacs doing the bidding of a madman in a cave.

The conspiracy theorists crave *more*. They need to believe in outrageously complicated plans involving our own government. They have to buy into theories about remote-controlled airplanes hitting the twin towers, missiles striking the Pentagon, and Flight 93 landing in Cleveland. They have to concoct conspiracies involving literally thousands of people, all acting in concert to fool the world.

On some strange level that's well beyond the ken of most logical minds, the conspiracy theorist takes some kind of psychological and emotional comfort in believing in the most complex, most outlandish scenario imaginable. If you can fixate on the illogical, the ludicrous, and the beyond ridiculous, you don't need to worry so much about the harsh realities of the world as we know it. You can live in a cocoon of paranoia, obsessing about Bush and Cheney and the rest of the Illuminati and their fictitious roles in the 9/11 attacks, instead of focusing your attention on the realities of a very scary world.

Consider the popularity of *Loose Change*, perhaps the most factually challenged documentary I've ever seen. (I also watched the updated version, *Loose Change: 2nd Edition*. It wasn't any better. I haven't watched *Loose Change: Final Cut*, released in November 2007, because life is too short to watch yet another version of a film with more holes than Pebble Beach. Besides, I'm waiting for the release of *Loose Change: We Were Just Kidding*.) This is an amateurish piece of panic-peddling nonsense riddled with half-truths, rehashed rumors, and implausible innuendo—yet it became a big hit on DVD and online.

If I went into all of the problems with *Loose Change* in this book, there wouldn't be any room to talk about deadly Jager Bombs and psychic hucksters and the "Clinton Body Count"—so we'll just spotlight a few of the holes in the film.

1. One of filmmaker Dylan Avery's favorite techniques is to present raw news footage from the morning of 9/11, when things were still developing and nobody was really sure what in God's name was happening to our world. Avery presents preliminary reports from correspondents working for CNN and Fox News and various local channels at the scenes of the three tragedies, as well as "eyewitness" accounts, as evidence of the conspiracies and cover-ups. Reporters and anchors talk of "explosions" at the World Trade Center. Regular folks talk about seeing planes that didn't look like commercial airliners.

So what? In a breaking news story of this magnitude, you'll almost always have early reports that eventually need to be corrected—and eyewitness accounts that turn out to be less than accurate. Hell, if you interview six people who witnessed a bar fight a few minutes after the fight ends, they're likely to give you six different versions of what went down. Do you think you're not going to get conflicting preliminary reports about what happened in lower Manhattan or at the Pentagon or in the skies above Pennsylvania on the morning of September 11?

True, a few eyewitnesses thought they saw noncommercial airliners flying into the World Trade Center. Then again, thousands of eyewitnesses *did* identify the planes as commercial aircraft. Not to mention the video footage that clearly shows these were passenger planes.

2. *Loose Change* quotes one Karl Schwarz as saying the engine at the Pentagon was from an A-3 Skywarrior. What the film fails to note is that Schwarz is an infamous conspiracy theorist and that he misidentified the type of engine that *would* be used with an A-3, had an A-3 been deployed, which was not the case.

3. In another segment, we're told that Charles Burlingame of the United States Navy was part of an exercise that simulated what it would be like if a commercial plane crashed into a building. *Loose Change* goes on to inform us that Burlingame took a job with American Airlines in 2000, less than a year before an American Airlines Boeing 757 crashed into the Pentagon.

Reality: Burlingame joined American Airlines in 1979, not 2000. He was on reserve assignment with the Pentagon until 1996—but he retired from the navy four years before the alleged exercise was said to have taken place.

4. *Loose Change* states as fact that Osama bin Laden was treated at the American Hospital in Dubai on July 4, 2001, and was visited by a CIA agent. There's absolutely no proof of this. The hospital and the CIA denied the rumor.

5. Sometimes the narration clearly contradicts the footage onscreen. We're told that explosions can clearly be seen detonating "20 to 30 stories" below the point of impact on the Trade Center towers—but the footage shows no such thing. We see debris shooting outward, which is what naturally occurs when a structural collapse is taking place.

In another instance, we're told there was a crash at the Pentagon "without a single scratch on the lawn," when that's clearly not the case.

6. According to *Loose Change*, the "official" explanation for the lack of debris at the Pentagon was that American Airlines Flight 77 and all its passengers "vaporized." No such explanation was ever offered. In fact, parts of the plane were recovered, and officials on the scene after the crash have told horrifying stories of finding body parts.

7. Avery also advocates perhaps the loopiest 9/11 conspiracy theory of them all: that Flight 93 never crashed in Pennsylvania, because it landed safely.

As we have already noted, you'll often see "first draft" reports during breaking news events that turn out not to be true. At one point on the morning of September 11, 2001, the Web site for a Cincinnati television station posted a link to an Associated Press story that erroneously mentioned United Flight 93 landing at Cleveland-Hopkins Airport due to a bomb threat.

The report, like so many reports filed in the middle of one of the most confusing and complicated days in the history of journalism, was in error.

According to the documentary, United Flight 93 really did land in Cleveland—and there were some 200 passengers on that plane, and they were "quickly taken to an empty NASA Research Center."

The phone calls placed by United 93 passengers and flight attendants? Phony. The crash site? Bogus.

So I guess that means that more than a half-dozen years after 9/11, the passengers on United Flight 93—and the passengers on those other planes, if we're to believe missiles and noncommercial aircraft were deployed in the three other crashes—are all still squirreled away in some research facility. That means that hundreds of citizens from all walks of life, people with families and jobs and lives that seemed to be normal—they were either a part of the conspiracy or were swept up in the grandiose plot. And now they're living their lives on a compound somewhere—or they've all been murdered by their government.

And what, pray tell, is the motivation behind all these conspiracies?

According to *Loose Change*, it's gold.

"Rumor has it that over $160 billion in gold was stored in the World Trade Center," we're told—and that only a couple hundred million was ever recovered. The World Trade Center was brought down, a plane (missile?) crashed into the Pentagon, and another plane secretly landed in Cleveland while a fake crash was staged in Pennsylvania—and it was all part of a plan to steal a shitload of gold.

"Rumor has it"? Well, gee, why didn't you just say so in the first place? Now we've got something to work with!

Rosie O'Donnell's blogging style falls somewhere between haiku and what-the-heck-is-that. On the "R Blog," O'Donnell fills her Web site with videos and stream-of-consciousness ramblings on topics ranging from her favorite charitable causes to her personal adventures to the war in Iraq.

She's also weighed in on 9/11, both in her former capacity as cohost of *The View* and on her blog, as in this entry:

> at 5:30 p.m.
> 9 11 2001
> wtc7 collapsed
>
> for the third time in history
> fire brought down a steel building
> reducing it to rubble

hold on folks
here we go

- The fires in WTC 7 were not evenly distributed, so a perfect collapse was impossible.
- Silverstein said to the fire department commander, "the smartest thing to do is pull it."
- The roof of WTC 7 visibly crumbled and the building collapsed perfectly into its footprint.

On *The View*, when Elisabeth Hasselbeck asked O'Donnell if she believed the United States government had anything to do with 9/11, Rosie replied, "No, but I do believe it's the first time in history that fire melted steel."

All together now: "The steel didn't have to melt!"

Thanks so much.

Rosie continued: "I do believe that it defies physics for World Trade Center 7, which collapsed in on itself. It is impossible for the building to fall the way it did without explosives being involved."

For the record: I admire much of what Rosie O'Donnell has accomplished over the years. She has fought tirelessly for the rights of gay and lesbian parents, she has raised millions of dollars for worthy causes, and she's never afraid to speak her mind, consequences be damned.

That said, when it comes to the fall of WTC 7, she's full of shit and she's giving a platform to some urban legends that will not die.

The myth persists that WTC 7 was just standing there intact some eight hours after Tower 1 and Tower 2 were felled, when all of it sudden it collapsed, as if part of some planned detonation.

For a moment let's ignore the evidence and the factual timeline of the day and make the huge leap of faith that says this is what really happened—that explosives were secretly planted in WTC 7 by unknown forces and that it "collapsed perfectly into its footprint."

If that's the case, why would the conspirators wait eight hours to set off the explosion? Wouldn't it make more sense for WTC 7 to fall in the morning while the madness and chaos were in full force?

By late afternoon/early evening, the world media were focused on Ground Zero. Never in the history of humankind had so many people been tuned to one locale. That's when you're going to sneak in a little thing like the collapse of a building? Or are we to believe that something went wrong and somebody somewhere was pushing a button for eight hours before finally getting the damn thing to go off?

As they say on the talk radio shows, I'll hang up and wait for my answer.

◎

Let's try to clear up some of the myths contained in Rosie's comments, made on her blog and on *The View*.

I'm pretty sure I don't have to say, "The steel didn't have to melt" yet again, but hey, I just did it.

Beyond that, the collapse of the 47-story WTC 7 in no way "defies physics." Smoke and rubble obscured the view of WTC 7 for a while, but as we have seen from countless pictures and hours of video footage, and as investigators have reported, tens of thousands of tons of steel girders from WTC 1 and WTC 2 fell directly onto WTC 7. There was also major damage to the southwest corner and to at least the first 10 floors of the south face of the building.

There was a tremendous amount of diesel fuel stockpiled in the basement of WTC 7—and that fuel burned for several hours. Throughout the afternoon, visible flames raged on the 11th and 12th floors. Other fires caused significant damage on the 5th, 6th, and 7th floors. The damage was so severe that the New York City Fire Department suspended all rescue-and-recovery efforts in the immediate vicinity of WTC 7. Expectations were that the building would collapse sooner rather than later.

At around 5:20 P.M. on September 11, WTC 7 collapsed. Nobody near the scene reported hearing explosive devices. (Never mind the myriad logistical problems that would be involved in wiring WTC 7—or for that matter WTC 1 and WTC 2—with enough explosives to down the structure.) Investigators never found any evidence of explosive devices. Reports from literally dozens of agencies in the public and private sectors indicated that the building sustained massive structural damage from falling debris and that fires weakened the structure. Nobody ever found evidence of a controlled-demolition blast.

As for the "Silverstein" comment, Rosie is referring to Larry Silverstein, the real estate developer who owned WTC 7.

First, *Pull it* is not an expression used by explosives demolition teams. It's used when a structure has been deliberately weakened— teams attach heavy cables to the building and "pull" it down, as if felling a tree.

Second, the owner of the building that's in flames does not have the authority to call for a building's demolition. That decision rests with the fire chief and other such authorities.

As a spokesperson for Silverstein later explained, Silverstein was simply relating a conversation he had had with the fire department in which they agreed that for the safety of all concerned, the best thing would be to pull *the firefighters* from the building. There was never any "directive" from Silverstein to bring down WTC 7. There are, however, dozens of solid press reports from that day quoting firefighters as saying that by 3 P.M., the consensus was that WTC 7 was going to collapse and the decision was made to get all personnel out of there.

But even if Silverstein did tell the fire chief to "pull the building," does that mean the owner of the building and the fire department were in on the conspiracy to destroy the World Trade Center? Are we to believe they had already installed explosives at some prior date and in the middle of the 9/11 madness publicly decided to "pull" the building? Why?

The footage of WTC 7 "suddenly" collapsing in "perfect" fashion—which does not show a perfect collapse at all—seemed so startling at the time that many immediately assumed it had to be rigged with explosives, but this doesn't follow the thinking of even the craziest 9/11 conspiracy theories. One can at least fathom the sick "logic" of a demented scenario that has some unseen forces planting explosives in the World Trade Center on the morning of a business day, thus causing a horrific, unspeakable disaster. Thousands are killed, a city and a country are thrown into chaos, and we thirst for revenge.

But what would be the purpose of demolishing WTC 7 more than eight hours after the initial attacks? There weren't any people in the building at that point. Why would the terrorists risk getting caught by exploding an empty, damaged WTC 7 while the whole world was watching?

I believe Rosie O'Donnell wants to know the truth. I believe the best way for her to learn this truth would be for her to get in touch with some of the firefighters who were at WTC 7 on the afternoon of 9/11, and perhaps some structural engineers. I believe they can clear up the misconceptions she has about the events of that day.

The Conspiracy Theorist (CT) says: "The World Trade Center was destroyed by explosives."

RR says: "The World Trade Center was destroyed by planes damaging the buildings' structure and by subsequent fires that significantly weakened the steel support columns."

CT: "Remote-controlled planes destroyed the World Trade Center."

RR: "Wait a minute—I thought it was a planned demolition. Now you're saying remote-controlled aircraft were involved? So did the remote-controlled planes simply distract us from the real culprit—the planned demolition? In any case, despite a few erroneous reports from faraway eyewitnesses, it's clear from video news footage and still photos that commercial aircraft slammed into the towers."

CT: "No, the passenger planes were diverted to a secret location."

RR: "Where? If that's the case, what happened to all the people on those planes? Were they part of the conspiracy, or were they victims of the conspiracy? If the passengers were taken to secret facilities, have they been living in those facilities for the better part of a decade? If the conspirators had no hesitation about murdering thousands of people in the towers, why would they keep the passengers alive? So does that mean some sort of mass execution took place in a government facility?"

CT: "The Pentagon was struck by a missile, not a plane."

RR: "Then why did we see pieces of a Boeing passenger jet? Why did forensic investigators say they identified body parts of dozens of passengers as well as the murderous hijackers? What about the recovery of the black box? If someone fired the missile—who would that be, exactly? From where was the missile launched? Shouldn't you have some evidence of something related to a missile attack before stating it as fact? And if it *was* a missile, what happened to Flight 77? Just how many thousands of government workers and civilians are in on this conspiracy, anyway?"

CT: "The holes in the Pentagon aren't big enough to accommodate the wingspan of a Boeing 757."

RR: "As experts have pointed out, this wasn't a *Road Runner* cartoon. A plane crashing into a reinforced building like the Pentagon isn't going to leave a friggin' silhouette. The truth: neither wing reached the building. Both were impacted and damaged before the bulk of the plane hit the Pentagon. The left wing was ripped off and smashed when it hit the ground, and the right wing—being made of material not as resistant as the Pentagon—shattered on impact."

CT: "How could a Boeing 757 damage only the outside wall of the Pentagon?"

RR: "That's not what happened. After crashing into a two-foot-thick, reinforced outer wall, the plane still caused damage to all five rings of the Pentagon."

CT: "Thousands of Jews in New York were alerted to the attacks beforehand, and they stayed home from work on 9/11."

RR: "Can you name one person who was given the advance word? Because I can give you the names of many Jews who were killed in New York on 9/11. The airplanes crashing into the towers did not discriminate on the basis of race, faith, or gender."

CT: "People with insider knowledge of the attacks purchased 'put' options on the airlines, knowing the stocks would plummet after 9/11."

RR: "Now we're bringing more people into the circle of the conspiracy. So we're to believe that a number of financial people had prior knowledge of the attacks—and rather than alert the authorities or the media, they rubbed their hands together and said, 'Time to make some money!' Really?

"It's true that there was some unusual trading—but in each case, investigators found no evidence of insider trading. For example, a single American company was responsible for 95 percent of the 'puts' on United Airlines on September 6. The Securities and Exchange Commission determined that this incident, as well as others, was in no way connected to the events of 9/11.

"But of course the SEC is in on the conspiracy, right?"

CT: "A study proved that cell phones don't work from high altitudes, which means the calls from United Flight 93 were faked using voice-morphing technology."

RR: "The study you're citing found problems with a specific brand of cell phone at a specific height. Passengers on Flight 93 used a variety of cell phone brands—as well as Air Fones, which of course *do* work at high altitudes. As for the whole voice-morphing thing— you've got to be kidding. Are we to believe that actors were hired to portray passengers as well as their loved ones? And that relatives and spouses of passengers were lying when they said they talked to people on the plane? They're all in on the conspiracy? Wow!"

CT: "If Flight 93 crashed in Pennsylvania, what happened to the so-called bodies?"

RR: "The *Washington Post* said approximately 1,500 'mostly scorched samples of human tissue' were found at the crash site. But I suppose the *Post*—the same newspaper that investigates potential crime and corruption at the highest levels of the U.S. government on a regular basis—is in on the conspiracy and is protecting the traitors."

CT: "The United States government engineered the attacks of 9/11 and participated in a mass cover-up of the truth."

RR: "This cover-up would have to include the Bush administration; the thousands of journalists who covered the attacks and the subsequent investigations; the New York City Fire and Police Departments; all the engineers and scientists and investigators who have officially found that airplanes operated by hijackers were the cause of the four crashes; the NASA employees who allegedly housed all the passengers that were on those four planes, and/or the passengers themselves; the New York City Port Authority; hundreds if not thousands of Pentagon employees; the FBI; the CIA; Rudy Giuliani; the Federal Aviation Administration; dozens of air traffic controllers; hundreds of other airport employees; family members that claimed they received calls from passengers aboard hijacked planes; the technical wizards who faked those calls; the criminal masterminds who sneaked into the towers and installed all those explosive charges; the evil geniuses that operated those remote-controlled planes that slammed into the towers; the traitors that launched the missile that blasted into the Pentagon; the Federal Emergency Management Agency; the volunteer workers at Ground Zero; the firefighters and cops from across the country who helped out at Ground Zero; and the many, many, many others who would have had to keep silent all these years about their participation in the most wide-ranging and nefarious conspiracy in the history of modern civilization."

If I'm wrong about this, you tell me how the conspiracy can remain hidden without the participation of *all* of the above groups of human beings.

One last question, this one about the 9/11 conspiracy detectives themselves: if they're actually onto something, why is the government allowing *them* to live when it has so casually and callously murdered so many others?

2

THE CLINTON KILL COUNT

Is it time to add one more name to the growing and stag-
gering Clinton body count? I don't know, but the fact that
such questions are not even raised in polite media com-
pany is not a good sign in a supposedly free society.

—Internet conspiracy theorist, blogging about
the latest so-called victim of Bill Clinton

O f all the smears, unfounded allegations, unseemly rumors,
and black-hearted lies perpetuated on Bill and Hillary Clinton over the last two decades, none is more unconscionable than
the so-called Clinton Body Count—the extensive list of people who
knew the Clintons and died under supposedly "mysterious circumstances."

This crap started up in the early 1990s, when some hatemon-
gers started compiling lists of Clinton associates who had died. (A
New York Times article traced the origins of the Clinton Body Count
list to an Indiana attorney named Linda Thompson, who had
founded a right-wing group called American Justice Federation,
which sounds like it should include the Green Lantern and the
Flash among its members.) By August 2000 there were dozens of
names on the list—and not one piece of tangible evidence that even

came close to reaching the level of a plausible rumor, let alone an actual indictment.

"Here is the latest body count we have," reads the lead on a piece of nonsense attributed to the "Ether Zone Staff," whoever the hell they are.

"All of these people have been connected with the Clintons in some form or another. We have not included any deaths that could not be verified or connected to the Clinton scandals."

Ooh, way to practice responsible journalism.

"All deaths are listed chronologically by date."

As opposed to chronologically by name, I suppose.

"This list is current and accurate to the best of our knowledge..."

Accurate? *Accurate*?!

If this is the best of their knowledge, I'd hate to see the *worst* of their alleged knowledge.

Here's a typical sampling of what you get when you peruse a Clinton Body Count list:

Susan Coleman. Rumors were circulating in Arkansas of an affair with Bill Clinton. She was found dead with a gunshot wound ... death was an apparent suicide.

Vincent Foster. A White House deputy counsel and long-time personal friend of Bill and Hillary's. Found on July 20, 1993, dead of a gunshot wound to the mouth—a death ruled suicide. Many theories on this case!

C. Victor Raiser. This former National Finance Co-Chairman of Clinton for President ... died in a suspicious private plane crash in Alaska. No cause determined.

Jim McDougal. Bill and Hillary friend, banker, political ally, sent to prison for 18 felony convictions. A key Whitewater witness, dies of a heart attack on March 8, 1998. As of this writing allegations that he was given an injection of the diuretic lasix have not been denied or confirmed.

And so it goes. You list someone who knew the Clintons, you record the way in which the person died, and you try to tie it all up in a ribbon of innuendo.

A piece of DVD hackwork titled *The Clinton Chronicles: An Investigation into the Alleged Criminal Activities of Bill Clinton* was released in 1994. The Reverend Jerry Falwell appeared in the "documentary" and also produced a lengthy infomercial for the film in which he spoke with a silhouetted journalist who said he feared for his life because he was getting too close to "the truth" about the Clinton Body Count. It was later revealed that the "journalist" was in fact the guy who produced the video.

Years later, Falwell admitted he had no idea if any of the allegations in *The Clinton Chronicles* were true. Sadly, he never apologized for the part he played in promoting the nasty piece of propaganda.

James McDougal had a heart condition. He died of a heart attack. An investigation turned up no evidence of foul play.

Vincent Foster's death is one of the most extensively investigated suicides in modern history. Don't you think a journalist for the *Washington Post* or the *Wall Street Journal* would want to uncover some piece of evidence suggesting Foster was murdered? Yet nobody ever found any credible information that it was anything other than a suicide.

There was nothing "suspicious" about the plane crash that claimed the life of C. Victor Raiser. The National Transportation Safety Board ruled that the cause of the crash was pilot error during conditions of poor visibility.

Susan Coleman was a law student of Clinton's. She killed herself. There's no proof she ever had an affair with Clinton.

◎

The Clinton Body Count resurfaced in 2007 after Hillary Clinton announced she was running for president.

"THINK ABOUT IT FIRST!" reads the e-mail.

> All of the folks [listed below] are indeed dead and it might all just be a tragic coincidence—but I wouldn't want to be on their list of associates, just to be on the safe side!!!!
>   SO YOU MIGHT VOTE FOR HILLARY? THINK ABOUT IT FIRST. . . .
> This is what happens when you have dirt on the Clintons.

What follows is a rehash of the same names and slimy semi-allegations about the deaths of various people associated with Clinton-related scandals and alleged scandals.

For anyone who believes there's some validity to a conspiracy theory that would involve Bill Clinton orchestrating shootings, robberies, plane and helicopter crashes, traffic homicides, and murders disguised as suicides, a couple of questions:

1. Why does the Clinton Body Count stop around the year 2000? Is he on hiatus, a la Kevin Costner's character in *Mr. Brooks*?
2. If Clinton was so intent on wiping out enemies, how did Monica Lewinsky, Rush Limbaugh, Ann Coulter, Linda Tripp, Kenneth Starr, and others escape his wrath?

3

THE CONSPIRACY THAT WON'T DI

I suspect not only Prince Charles but Prince Philip, who is a racist. It is absolutely black-and-white, horrendous murder.

—Among the more ludicrous and patently false blusterings from Mohammed al Fayed concerning the deaths of his son and Princess Diana

Princess Grace of Monaco. James Dean. Jackson Pollock. Lisa "Left Eye" Lopes. Harry Chapin. Steve Allen. Isadora Duncan. Sam Kinison. Jayne Mansfield.

Princess Diana.

That's just a partial list of 20th-century pop figures that died in automobile accidents. It stands to reason that a number of celebrities would be killed in car wrecks simply because a lot of *people* die that way. Some 43,000 Americans die each year in vehicle accidents—more than the total number of deaths from firearms, falls, suffocation, fires, drowning, poisoning, and plane crashes put together.

Let's put it this way: Ask any 10 people you know if they knew someone who was killed in a car accident, and 8 or 9 will say yes. But perhaps only 1 of those 10 will say they knew somebody who was killed in a fire or a plane crash.

When someone is killed in a car wreck, of course it's a terrible tragedy—but it's certainly not unusual, and it rarely means there was foul play involved. Accidents happen every day, every hour, virtually every minute.

Yet more than a decade after Princess Diana and two men were killed in one of the most public and publicly chronicled auto accidents in history, there are those who swear she was murdered by a coalition of evil forces who conspired to snuff her out for any number of reasons.

The conspiracy theories began to mushroom before the crash scene was cleared.

"Our website, Conspire.com, received its first e-mail on the subject—asserting that Di was killed by MI-5 [sic]—within minutes of the initial news bulletins of the car crash on Aug. 31" is the claim of one conspiracy site.

That's amazing, given that those first news bulletins didn't even have solid information on Diana's condition, let alone whether she had died. And of course if you have evidence that one of the world's most famous women has been assassinated, you don't contact the authorities or the mainstream media—you e-mail a conspiracy Web site. That'll blow the lid off the whole thing!

According to *Time* magazine, on the day after Diana died, Egyptian writer Mohammad Hassanein Haykal pondered, "A conspiracy-type question arises here . . . was something arranged to kill the most famous lovers of the closing years of the 20th century?"

"A day or two later," according to the *Time* article, "Libyan strongman Muammar Gaddafi weighed in during an official broadcast, claiming: 'British and Secret Services mounted and executed the assassination of the Princess of Wales and the Arab citizen who were planning to get married.'" Gaddafi provided no evidence to back up this assertion.

A good percentage of the public has remained skeptical about the official version of events.

In 1998 a London newspaper poll found that 27 percent believed Diana had been murdered. A year later, a BBC poll found that 31 percent of the British population thought Diana's death was not an accident.

On the sixth anniversary of Diana's death, the *Sunday Express* published a poll that found 49 percent of Brits believed there was some kind of "cover-up" in the case.

In a CBS news poll in 2004, some 76 percent of Americans said they believe "we will never know the whole truth" about Diana's death.

Noel Botham's *The Murder of Princess Diana*, which was turned into a Lifetime Original Movie in August 2007, purports to blow the lid off "The cover-up of the century!" but does little more than ask wildly speculative questions such as "Did Diana's international campaign against landmines create a deadly conflict within the CIA?"

I don't know, pal—you tell me.

Leading the conspiracy charge is Mohammed al Fayed, the billionaire father of Dodi Fayed, the man who was seeing Diana at the time and was also killed in the wreck. Although some reports say the Di-Dodi romance was a fling that was already flickering out, al Fayed is convinced not only that was his son going to marry Di, but also that she was pregnant with his child.

Over the last 10 years, the grieving father has devoted much of his life and a considerable chunk of his fortune to proving the so-called accident was orchestrated by the royal family—yet despite all that money and clout, he hasn't come close to proving a thing.

Here's al Fayed's version of the chain of events that led to the fatal crash—a version echoed, with some variations, by many conspiracy Web sites.

Prince Philip and Prince Charles were supposedly horrified at the notion of the mother of the future king of England marrying a Muslim and giving her sons a half-brother who also would be Muslim.

The only solution: murder.

Henri Paul, the acting security chief for the Ritz-Carlton in Paris, who was behind the wheel of Di's car that fateful night, was secretly working for the MI6—the British foreign Secret Intelligence Service. He was in on the plan.

When Paul entered the Pont de l'Alma tunnel, a Fiat Uno driven by a hired hit man deliberately crashed into the Mercedes, setting off the deadly crash. Ah, but what Henri Paul didn't know was that he, too, was supposed to be killed in the crash. Turns out he was nothing but a patsy for the conspirators. (Bodyguard Trevor Rees-Jones, who apparently was not in on the plot, survived the crash.)

Some conspiracy theorists claim that Diana faked her own death. Others say the paparazzi were paid off to chase the Mercedes into the tunnel and facilitate the crash. There's even a theory that says *Dodi* was the real target, and the death of Diana was only the greatest diversionary tactic ever.

My theory is even crazier than any of the above.

I think it was an accident.

Those who fixate on the supposed scandal of Diana marrying Dodi and having a child with him seem to be forgetting some important points:

- Diana had known Dodi for only six weeks. Close friends of hers say there was no indication she planned to get serious with him, let alone marry him.
- Diana wasn't pregnant. That was the official finding of the autopsy. (Aha! The royals got to the coroner as well!)
- Diana was no longer a member of the royal family. What would it matter if the ex-wife of Prince Charles married Dodi? So in 20 or 30 years, when her fortysomething son, Prince William, ascended to the throne, his stepfather (assuming Di and Dodi were still together) would be Muslim and by that time he might have had a Muslim stepbrother? So what?

- The conspiracy-fantasy laid out by al Fayed and others incorporates at least two members of the Royal family, key personnel within the British Secret Intelligence Service, al Fayed's own employee Henri Paul, and perhaps others. And all this time, nobody who was on the inside has breathed a credible word about this plot?
- How did the driver of that mysterious white Fiat know which route the Mercedes was going to take? There are numerous ways to go from the Ritz-Carlton to Dodi's flat in Paris. Were there mysterious white Fiats planted along every possible route?
- What about the alcohol and drugs in Henri Paul's system? Is that another piece of evidence manufactured by the conspirators to mask the "real" cause of death?
- The coroner overseeing the inquest into the accident said in 2007 there was "not a shred of evidence" of a conspiracy. He urged al Fayed to produce tangible evidence. None was forthcoming. Instead, al Fayed continues to make wild accusations backed by nothing but his own emotions and mad fantasies.
- A three-year investigation into the case by British authorities yielded an 832-page report. The inquiry found that the driver was intoxicated and traveling at dangerous speeds when he lost control of a powerful car with which he was not familiar. In the words of the report, it was a "tragic accident."
- A two-year investigation conducted by the French, with more than 30 detectives interviewing some 300 witnesses, yielded a 6,000-page report. The finding: it was an accident.

Yes, I'm aware of the letter Diana wrote to her brother expressing fears that she might be done in via a suspicious car accident. When the conspiracy theorists pounce on that letter as proof of a plot—which of course it is not—they conveniently avoid mentioning that months prior to receiving that letter in 1996, the Earl of Spencer had written to Diana, expressing hopes and prayers that she was getting help for her "mental problems."

Diana was a troubled soul. She once made the unsubstantiated claim that someone had tried to take a shot at her in London. Another time, she expressed fears that she would be killed in a helicopter crash that would look like an accident but would really be murder. Just because she entertained a paranoid fantasy about her ex-husband killing her (not because of Dodi, whom she had yet to meet when she wrote the letter, but because it would "clear the way" for Charles to marry Camilla Parker Bowles) doesn't mean such a plot was ever hatched or carried out.

From the French police to Scotland Yard, the investigation into the death of Princess Diana is perhaps the most extensive and thorough probe of its kind. Because this was one of the world's most famous and beloved figures, investigators have spared no expense on this case. Literally hundreds of law enforcement authorities, medical experts, and witnesses have participated in one investigation or another.

And yet we still have not a single substantial piece of evidence that anyone, let alone the royals and the British Secret Intelligence Service, conspired to kill Diana and Dodi.

4

THE KENNEDY ASSASSINATION, 1999 EDITION

John F. Kennedy, Jr., made one grave mistake. He trusted the presidential campaign officials of Albert Gore, Jr. . . .

—Excerpt from an essay on the Internet arguing that
John F. Kennedy Jr. was assassinated

John F. Kennedy Jr. and Princess Diana were arguably the two most iconic pop culture celebrities of the 1990s. Diana was killed in a car crash in 1997, and Kennedy was killed in a small-plane crash in 1999—but the conspiracy theories about their deaths live on and probably will never die.

One can at least understand why some conspiracy theorists would find rich material in the circumstances surrounding Diana's death—but Kennedy's plane crash, while terribly sad, was a pretty straightforward accident, right? We all know that Kennedy; his wife, Carolyn; and his wife's sister, Lauren, were killed when Kennedy lost control of his single-engine plane—end of story.

Yeah, right.

Here was the reaction on the Rense.com Web site after the National Transportation Safety Board released its official report citing pilot error as the cause of the crash:

> Note—we rate this "final, official" report of "pilot error" as the cause of the JFK, Jr., plane crash right up there with that outrage called the Warren Commission Report, and at least as disgusting as the NTSB's claim that TWA 800 crashed because of a "center fuel tank spark and explosion." Nearly all major evidence and circumstance of the JFK crash point to the opposite conclusion of "pilot error."

The conspiracy site North Star Zone has a home page linking to articles with headlines such as "Ten Lies Your Doctor Told You," "Pearl Harbor: The Great Deception," "When They Kill a Pope," and "The Truth Behind the Virginia Tech Massacre." (It was "hypnotic mind control. Including [the killer], 33 were killed. 33 is the highest degree of Freemasonry one can attain, and is used as an Illuminati signal passing a message to 'those in the know' that one of their Manchurian Candidates has carried out his orders.")

Think of any major news event, assassination, or public tragedy of the last several decades, and the North Star Zone is there to explain what *really* happened—which is never the "official" version of events.

"Was JFK Jr. Murdered?" the site asks.

"Many unbiased researchers have spent the years since JFK Jr.'s July 1999 plane crash and untimely death, carefully gathering the facts about what really happened, and this investigation leads them to only one conclusion: MURDER, from a bomb placed aboard his aircraft. Their painstaking investigations reveal a massive cover-up by the controlled national media. They expose the false statements and lies that were fed to the apathetic and gullible American public, who only too gladly will swallow the swill dished out daily by the managed news and disinformation networks."

"Swallow the Swill"—I believe that was one of the test slogans for the Fox News Channel, but they settled on "Fair and Balanced."

Despite the grandiose claims in the introduction about a "murder" and "massive cover-up," the article offers no proof whatsoever of either bombshell.

"Who would have killed JFK Jr.? The same people that murdered his father," states the article. "The International Bankers, the Shadow Government, the One Worlders, the Illuminati, the secret societies, those who will not hesitate to get rid of anyone who gets in their way in building their socialistic One World Government."

Wow, that's an awful lot of people working together in a conspiracy of silence. Doesn't anybody ever break ranks and spill the beans? Guess they'd be killed immediately if they tried, right?

As for that whole "One World Government" theory, what world are they talking about? Where is that taking place? Not on this planet.

So why exactly was John Jr. killed? Turns out he was going to turn *George* magazine into "a true political vehicle for change."

> Apparently he was in the process of documenting and proving with facts that . . . hidden forces, along with the international bankers and their operatives, the CIA, were responsible for the foul acts against his father . . . and his uncle RFK. . . . Several investigators have asserted that JFK Jr. was planning to announce he was running for president as a traditional Democrat, or even possibly as a third party independent candidate in the 2000 election.

The "article," and at this point we really do have to put the word *article* in quotation marks, points a finger at George W. Bush as someone who would "most naturally have an interest in the demise of JFK Jr." and makes the claim that "the FBI covered up the bombing of JFK Jr.'s plane." It goes on to say that if Kennedy had run for president, he would have "swept the field of presidential candidates. Conservatives and liberals, both could join together to support him."

Right. Rush Limbaugh, Sean Hannity, and Ann Coulter would have supported a John-John run for the presidency. Now we're really getting into fantasy territory.

Another essay on the same site makes the argument that Kennedy was "highly experienced" and that his trainers said he was "excellent." A page later, the author makes the unsubstantiated claim that there was a flight instructor on the plane (apparently the instructor's body mysteriously disappeared, and he had no family or friends to report him missing) and that the flight instructor "disappeared from the reports." A few paragraphs after lauding Kennedy's experience and skill as a pilot, the author states, "It is almost unthinkable that he would not have taken an instructor."

But if Kennedy did bring along an instructor, how did the instructor's body mysteriously vanish? I guess we're supposed to believe that while the official word was that Kennedy's plane had gone down and rescue/recovery efforts were under way, a secret team had already plucked the instructor's remains from the sea and had erased all traces of his existence in order to give more credence to the NTSB's bogus "pilot error" report.

Which had yet to be filed.

According to a DVD titled *The Assassination of JFK Jr.—Murder by Manchurian Candidate*, there is "overwhelming, jaw-dropping evidence of foul play in the death of John Kennedy Jr., all based on official government documents."

> The search of the crash site was delayed an incomprehensible 15 hours. There was, indeed, a flight instructor on the plane, whose body is missing. It is clear that someone on that plane committed suicide, shutting off the fuel control valve before plunging the plane into the sea. The prime suspect, George W. Bush, though very publicly running for president, disappeared the day of the murder and stayed missing for three days.

All of this "evidence" and more is presented via a "documentary" with production values that make the typical teenager's lip-synching-to-Beyoncé video on YouTube look like a production number from *Dreamgirls*.

The idea that George W. Bush would mastermind the murder of JFK Jr. is beyond ludicrous—but even if you were to buy into that insanity, it's simply not true that Bush "disappeared the day of the murder." As dozens of wire stories and newspaper articles reported, Bush was in Iowa on that Friday, making numerous campaign stops. Bush did take the weekend off from public campaign appearances—as had been planned—but by Monday morning, he was in Austin, Texas, publicly expressing sympathy for the Kennedy family.

In the meantime, Democratic candidate Al Gore canceled three campaign appearances for that Saturday out of respect for the Kennedy family—or was it because *he* was a part of the plot as well?

According to some conspiracy theorists, that's exactly the case. You see, Bush and Gore teamed up for this murder! Sigh.

Let's remember that by the time of Kennedy's tragic accident, Bush was a shoo-in for the Republican nomination. He had a presidential-sized security contingent and a pool of reporters assigned to cover him—even on his days off. The idea that the governor of Texas, who was the clear front-runner for his party's nomination for president, could fall off the radar for hours, let alone days, is just silly.

But not as silly as the DVD's assertion that Bush, Donald Rumsfeld, Dick Cheney, and Chairman of the Joint Chiefs of Staff Richard Myers were in a boat off Martha's Vineyard on the night of the crash, orchestrating Kennedy's assassination.

Not to mention the idea that either Kennedy, his wife, her sister, or the nonexistent instructor sabotaged the plane and then committed suicide.

Watching the DVD, I began to wonder if this was performance art. I mean, these people have to be kidding, right?

Sadly, I think they're serious.

◎

According to the NTSB's official report, a flight instructor offered to fly with Kennedy that night but Kennedy refused. We know this because the flight instructor is *still alive to be quoted in the report.*

Despite the claims of conspiracy theorists that Kennedy was an expert pilot, the truth is he was rated to fly under visual flight rules only. That means he did not have the expertise to fly a plane based only on cockpit instrument readings.

When the plane was about 35 miles west of Martha's Vineyard, Kennedy reportedly experienced a well-known phenomenon called "spatial disorientation." Even though his plane had begun descending, his instincts would have told him it was climbing—and "corrective" measures would actually make the situation much worse.

The NTSB found no evidence of an explosion or fire. No evidence of foul play.

Although the conspiracy theorists love to point out that conditions were clear that night, the truth is that while Kennedy received a weather report two hours before takeoff that provided a reasonable visibility forecast, pilots who took the same path taken by Kennedy on the night of the crash said conditions had turned hazy, resulting in "significantly reduced visibility."

Bob Stone, a Martha's Vineyard glider pilot with 40 years of experience, told the *Providence Journal-Bulletin*, "I've flown enough around this island to know that not only can those hazy conditions persist for days, that haze can pop at low levels almost instantly. When you're in it, down becomes up and up becomes down. It happens."

Of course, Stone was probably recruited by the Illuminati back in the 1950s to pose as a glider pilot for all those decades, just so he'd be in place to offer up that quote after the plan was carried out.

Dr. Bob Arnot, a veteran pilot and a reporter for NBC, took off from the same airport as Kennedy on the night of the crash. He told NBC's *Dateline* the air was extremely dark to the point of being "inky," and said he thought to himself that night that if someone wasn't experienced in reading instruments, they could run into serious trouble. (Remember, Kennedy wasn't licensed to fly the plane by cockpit readings.)

Then again, how can we believe someone who is part of the media conspiracy? Obviously the Pentagon got to Arnot.

The sad, not-sensational reality is that John Kennedy was a good but not great pilot who almost certainly lost control of his plane and lacked the experience and knowledge to save himself, his wife, and her sister.

II

THE MEDIA

5

IT'S A MEDIA BLACKOUT

If this case had been white-on-black crime, Al Sharpton and Jesse Jackson and their ilk would have descended on Knoxville like a swarm of angry bees.

—Country music star Charlie Daniels, commenting on the murder of a young white couple, allegedly at the hands of five black assailants

Like Nicole Brown Simpson and Ronald Goldman, like Laci Peterson and JonBenet Ramsey and so many others, Christopher Newsom and Channon Christian fall into that tragic category of people who became public figures only after they were murdered.

Nobody outside of their friends and family heard of them before they were murdered. Few outside the Knoxville, Tennessee, area knew about them even after they were murdered.

But in the weeks and months that followed the brutal killings, Newsom and Christian became a cause celebre—the poster couple for those who believe the mainstream media conspire to shy away from stories involving white victims and black criminals because they don't fit into our "game plan" for how race should be covered in the United States.

This theory, folks, is pure bullshit. We'll examine why it makes no sense in a bit, but first we'll take a look at the Newsom/Christian story.

Be warned in advance, some of these details are beyond grisly.

◎

In late spring 2007, I began receiving e-mails about a "mainstream media cover-up" of an alleged hate crime in Knoxville, Tennessee.

"Dear Mr. Roeper," the reader would say, "You're supposed to be a straight shooter and you're supposed to be someone who tells it like it is, but I'll bet you won't tell THIS story! Please read the e-mail below that was forwarded to me by a friend."

The e-mail in question:

Bet you $20 you didn't hear about this one on the national news.

The animals pictured below raped Christopher Newsom, cut off his penis, set him on fire and shot him several times. They forced his girlfriend, Channon Christian, to watch. Channon was then beaten and gang-raped...for four days...they cut off her breasts ...and murdered her.

Why hasn't this case received national coverage by the news media like the Duke 'rape' case?

Oh, that's right—the victims were white.

Why hasn't the NAACP, ACLU, New York Times, etc., called for an investigation?

Must be 'cause the victims were white.

Why hasn't the FBI been called in to investigate this as a hate crime?

Oh, that's right—the victims were white.

Nearly every e-mail I received about the case mentioned the Duke case, in which three white lacrosse players were thrust into the national spotlight when a black exotic dancer accused them of raping her (all charges were later dropped). Most e-mails referenced

Rev. Al Sharpton and Rev. Jesse Jackson and wondered why they were silent about the Knoxville story.

All indicted the mainstream media for "ignoring" the story.

Country music star and flag-waving patriot Charlie Daniels wrote about the case in the "Soapbox" section of his Web site. He repeated the details about the victims being mutilated and implied that mainstream news organizations such as the television networks, the *New York Times,* and the (Nashville) *Tennessean* weren't reporting on the case because "the five perpetrators who have all been arrested were black."

Writes Daniels: "A free press is one of our most precious rights and a selective press is one of our most dangerous realities. To suppress or ignore one of the most hideous murders of the decade is asinine and reeks of political correctness and agenda-driven formats."

Then again, it's also important to get the facts straight and to have some evidence of a cover-up before claiming one exists.

A few corrections here. While no sane person could even begin to argue that the murders of Newsom and Christian were anything but horrific, the truth is that neither victim was mutilated—nor was Christian dismembered or her body stuffed into five different trash bags, as many Internet accounts claimed.

The known details of the case are grotesque as it is; embellishing them to serve the cause of an argument is unconscionable. Repeating those embellishments as facts is just lazy.

Here's what we know, based on police accounts and sound reportage by reputable sources.

On January 6, 2007, Newsom, 23, and Christian, 21, were leaving an apartment complex in Knoxville when they were accosted by carjackers who took their vehicle and abducted them at gunpoint. They were taken to a rental house, where both were repeatedly raped.

After several hours, Newsom was shot and his body set afire and dumped near some railroad tracks. Christian remained alive for several more hours before she was killed, her body dumped in a trash can.

These were two innocent, decent, terrific young people just starting their lives. It's almost incomprehensible that human beings—go ahead and call them animals if you want—would do such things to them. I'm considered a liberal, but if the five people charged with these crimes are guilty and you told me tonight that all five had just been crushed to death by a meteor that fell from the sky, I'd say they got off easy and I wouldn't lose a second of sleep.

◎

When the murders occurred, local media in Tennessee covered the case responsibly and with appropriate weight.

"Bodies of missing couple found" was the state Associated Press wire story on January 10, 2007.

"3 men in custody after Tennessee couple found dead" was the headline two days later.

"2 ex-cons, 2 other men in custody in carjacking, rape, slaying of Tennessee couple" was the next headline.

And so it went, with the local media covering each arrest and providing the grisly details without sensationalizing the case.

But somewhere between winter and spring, the story took on a life of its own, with right-wing journalists, conservative bloggers, anonymous e-mailers, and (most regrettably) white supremacists all claiming the story had been ignored or buried by the mainstream media because the victims were white and the alleged criminals were black.

In May 2007 ultraconservative columnist Michelle Malkin repeated the "unconfirmed reports" about sexual mutilation on her video blog and said police found Christian's body in "five separate trash bags." Malkin trotted out references to the Duke case and to the well-publicized murders of James Byrd Jr. (a black man killed by white supremacists) and Matthew Shepard (a gay student killed in an apparent hate crime), then noted the mainstream media "hasn't asked any questions" about the Knoxville case.

An attractive white couple murdered by five thugs doesn't seem to fit any political agenda. It's not a "useful crime." Reverse the races and just imagine how the national press would cover the story of a young black couple brutally murdered by five white assailants. The details of the crime make it a national story . . . but somehow, it ain't fit to print or air.

A white supremacist who organized a rally in Knoxville to protest black-on-white crime told the *Knoxville News Sentinel* the murders were "covered up" by a media that supports "white genocide."

In the *National Review*, Jack Dunphy made yet another comparison to the Duke case and stated, "The murders of Channon Christian and Christopher Newsom are known to almost no one outside Tennessee. Why? It's simple: the . . . suspects accused of killing Christian and Newsom are blacks from the inner city of Knoxville."

As someone who has worked in a newsroom for nearly two decades, including a stint as a news reporter before becoming a news columnist, I'll try to explain why the Duke case received so much more play from the mainstream than the Knoxville murders.

First you have the fact that while the Duke lacrosse team isn't exactly nationally known, Duke University is one of the most famous athletic and academic powerhouses in the world and is often held up as the embodiment of the privileged collegiate life. For everyone who admires Duke, there's somebody who hates Duke for its very Dukeness.

So here you have a group of golden boys who hire exotic dancers to work a party in a private residence—and one of the strippers says she was raped, beaten, and sodomized. An ugly, misogynist e-mail authored by one Duke player surfaces. The local district attorney exploits the case as a star-making opportunity. (Instead, it becomes a career-shattering debacle.) We hear reports that racial epithets were hurled that night. There's much talk about the simmering racial and social class tensions in Durham, North Carolina, between the local "townies" and the rich-kid students.

Of course it's a national story. It's a Tom Wolfe novel, for crying out loud. You've got race, class, sex, violence, ambition, power, greed—all the elements of a classic, albeit lurid, sensational tale.

The story in Knoxville is hellish and stomach churning—but the harsh reality is that maximum-security facilities around the country are jammed full with thugs and lowlifes who have committed equally terrible crimes. As awful as this story is, it would be difficult for one to make the case, based on the facts, that it "deserves" ongoing national coverage.

Malkin argues that because some of the suspects could receive the death penalty, this was a national story. Well, there are more than 3,300 inmates on death row in this country, yet only a tiny percentage of those death row convictions were national stories. If the networks, the *New York Times*, and CNN devoted all their time and resources to the coverage of particularly heinous murders across the United States, there wouldn't be time to report on anything else in the world.

Critics want to know why the Knoxville case isn't a "hate crime." If those animals didn't have hate in their hearts, who does?

Part of the problem, I believe, is the terminology. It would be more appropriate and accurate to categorize some acts as "crimes of bigotry" or, when accurate, "race crimes." Most rational, decent "civilians" look at any violent crime and assume the perpetrator must have had hatred in his heart, when any veteran cop or crime reporter can tell you that the sad truth is, many criminals are utterly indifferent to their victims; they don't care about them enough to hate them.

In a *Chicago Sun-Times* story from June 25, 2007, psychologist, crime profiler, and crime-book author John Philpin said that one type of psychopathic killer regards his victims as "less than people. They're something to get rid of."

Incidentally, that story ran after a man named Christopher Vaughn was charged with shooting his wife, Kimberly, and their three children in the family's SUV. Vaughn claimed his wife had shot him and he had run away, only to return and find his wife and children all dead.

For two weeks, Kimberly's family maintained she would never hurt her children. There were all kinds of stories about troubles in the marriage, about Christopher taking Kimberly to a gun range, about Christopher's occasionally volatile behavior. Investigators patiently pieced their case together, waiting for key pieces of evidence (for example, tests determined there was no gun residue on Kimberly's hands). Police arrested Vaughn at a funeral home in Missouri on the morning of his family's burials.

Pretty dramatic stuff, right?

Yet it went almost unnoticed by the national media. The *Chicago Tribune* and *Chicago Sun-Times* played the story heavily, and it was a fixture on the local Chicago news—but other than a feature on Nancy Grace's crime-oriented show on CNN, it hardly made a blip on the national radar. There were no stories in the *New York Times* or the *Washington Post*, no national spotlight focused on these murders.

Why? Was there some sort of cover-up? Of course not. The Vaughn case simply wasn't that unusual in the sense of being a national story.

In the legal sense of the term, there has been no indication the Knoxville murders were racially motivated. Thus, no "hate crime." Authorities have repeatedly said there's no evidence of a hate crime—no reason to believe Newsom and Christian were specifically targeted because they were white.

"There is absolutely no proof of a hate crime," said a Knox County district attorney special counsel in an article in the *Chicago Tribune*.

> It was a terrible crime, a horrendous crime, but race was not a motive. We know from our investigation that the people charged in this case were friends with white people, socialized with white people, dated white people. So not only is there no evidence of any racial animus, there's evidence to the contrary.

Eventually the Knoxville case did become a national story—not because it was a hate crime, not because the country was mourning two fine young people, but because the story became a symbol of how the media supposedly cover race. Some people seem more outraged by the supposed liberal-media conspiracy than the fates of Channon Christian and Christopher Newsom.

One of the questions I never see addressed in any of the blogs or rants or e-mails is a simple one: Why?

Why would it be in the best interests of the mainstream media to ignore certain types of hate crime? You're saying we're that interested in pandering to a certain segment of the audience at the risk of alienating a larger percentage of readers/viewers?

For that matter, if there was no hate crime, what exactly were we supposed to dwell on for months and months? The horrible crimes were committed, the suspects were quickly rounded up, and they await trial. This was never like the Duke case, with so many layers of intrigue and drama, so many twists and turns. As a developing news story, there simply weren't that many developments once the arrests were made.

I'm also a little confused about which side the mainstream media are supposedly on. First we're told that we constantly favor stories involving missing white women such as Natalee Holloway and white children such as JonBenet Ramsey. Why don't we cover the stories of missing black women and murdered Hispanic children with equal gusto? We must be racist.

Now we're told we rush to cover white-on-black crime but we shy away from stories involving white victims and black criminals. We must be pandering to minorities.

So which is it? Are we talking about two separate conspiracies that would seem to cancel out each other?

Or maybe the secret cabals just meet in different rooms to hash these things out.

6

KATRINA AND THE WAVES OF MISINFORMATION

It doesn't take anything to start a rumor around here.

—Second Lieutenant Lance Cagnolatti of the Louisiana
National Guard, quoted by the *Los Angeles Times*
"at the height of the Superdome relief effort"
following Hurricane Katrina

If you believed all the stories of looting, assault, robbery, mayhem, manslaughter, rape, and murder in New Orleans following Hurricane Katrina, the city was like something straight out of the movie *Children of Men*—a postapocalyptic nightmare, hell on Earth.

Disasters and tragedies always bring out the best as well as the worst of humankind. You are who you are, to the 10th power.

In the case of Katrina, it seemed as if the worst was winning. The stories ranged from the disgusting to the horrific.

I received an e-mail from someone claiming to be related to a New Orleans resident. The resident told this person that a police boat had approached a young woman who was stranded on the roof of a house. The cops allegedly told the woman, "Show us your t—s!" as if this were Mardi Gras and not one of the worst disasters in the American history.

When the woman refused to comply, the police boat continued on.

At least according to the story I was told.

In the early days of the disaster, the mainstream media reported that post-flood New Orleans had essentially been overtaken by the criminal element.

On the Fox News Channel's *Hannity & Colmes* program on September 1, 2005, Alan Colmes said, "There are troubling reports tonight, coming from inside the city of New Orleans. There've been shootings. There are reports of people being robbed and raped. Shots have been fired at police officers. And gangs roam the streets at night in the darkness."

In a story that was picked up by hundreds of news outlets across the world, the Associated Press reported that in the early morning hours of September 1, shots had been fired at a military helicopter and that evacuation proceedings had been halted because of the gunfire.

"LOST CITY" was the headline in the *Chicago Sun-Times* that accompanied an AP wire story. "New Orleans in anarchy as rage, frustration grip desperate survivors."

The AP story began, "Storm victims were raped and beaten, fights and fires broke out, corpses lay out in the open, and rescue helicopters and law enforcement officers were shot at as flooded-out New Orleans descended into anarchy Thursday."

New Orleans police chief Eddie Compass was quoted as saying, "We have individuals who are getting raped; we have individuals who are getting beaten. Tourists are . . . getting preyed upon."

In an exchange with the Reverend Al Sharpton, MSNBC's Tucker Carlson said, "People are being raped. People are being murdered. People are being shot. Police officers being shot. Helicopters are being shot at. And that's one of the reasons people who need it aren't getting the aid tonight. There's no excusing that behavior."

Arthel Neville, a New Orleans native and the host of *A Current Affair*, told Fox News's Greta Van Susteren some stories bordering on the unfathomable.

NEVILLE: My cousin swam down Tulane Avenue. She says, "I can't take it here." There's snakes in the water, there's sharks in the water. She said, "I don't care."

VAN SUSTEREN: Really, sharks?

NEVILLE: I haven't seen them. I heard that. Snakes, you got to believe that. . . . One guy gets into a scuffle with a National Guardsman, takes the gun and kills the guardsman with the gun. Another guy, this is really sad, if there are any children in the room take them out of the room, a man rapes and kills a seven-year-old girl. About 10 guys, I don't know how many, but a group of guys turn around and beat this guy to death. This is just horrible. I cannot wrap my mind around how . . . a human person can be reduced to such animalistic behavior. I don't understand it.

The horror stories kept coming, one after another.

According to a French newspaper, some 1,200 people drowned inside a school.

A local blues singer told a Baton Rouge television station she had been raped and had witnessed alligators eating people before she commandeered a bus and drove a number of people to safety.

Chief Compass went on *The Oprah Winfrey Show* and said babies were being raped in the Superdome. Mayor Ray Nagin told Oprah of people who were "in that friggin' Superdome for five days watching dead bodies, watching hooligans killing people, raping people."

But after the first few days, the reports of mayhem seemed to just fade away. To be sure, New Orleans was still reeling from the overwhelming scope of the disaster, and crimes were committed, but there were few follow-ups offering further details concerning the rapes and the murders and the episodes of alligators eating people, like something out of a John Carpenter movie.

The conspiracy theorists said it was obvious the White House had placed the media under a cone of silence—ordering news organizations to pull back on the horror stories. This was no time to cause further panic in New Orleans; neither was it helping our image around the globe if the international media believed there was chaos in the streets of New Orleans and that thousands of Americans had turned into rabid animals.

The conspiracy was on.

Or not.

What really happened: once the media took some Responsibility Pills and reporters had the time and opportunity to start examining some of the more incredible stories, they were able to separate fact from urban legend.

I mean, come on. A woman saw alligators eating people just before she took control of a bus and drove a bunch of people to safety? I wouldn't believe that scene if I saw it in *Fantastic Four*.

Turns out everyone, from the mayor of New Orleans to the police chief to the host of *A Current Affair*, was repeating stories someone had told someone who had told someone else. In hindsight, it's easy to say that talk show hosts such as Winfrey and Van Susteren should have expressed more skepticism from the get-go, but that's not always the first reaction when you're hearing such mind-boggling tales of chaos and anarchy—especially when it's an authority figure telling the tales.

As the cleanup and restoration efforts in New Orleans continued, a number of mainstream news organizations and Internet investigators were disputing most of the worst stories, with the help of authorities.

"Katrina spawned rumors; media ran with them" was the headline in the *Philadelphia Inquirer* on September 28, 2005.

"Over five days . . . stories of unspeakable horror were reported around the world, by broadcast and cable TV, the BBC, the Associated Press, Reuters, web sites, and many newspapers" read the article, which went on to refute nearly all of the horror stories.

The New Orleans Police Department has no substantiated reports of rapes—no victims, and no eyewitnesses. There was a single homicide inside the Convention Center, and no murders inside the Superdome, according to the Louisiana Health and Human Services Department, which is overseeing the recovery of remains.

Officials who were prepared to remove hundreds of the dead from the shelters found 10 bodies in the Dome, four brought in from the streets and six of people who died on-site—four of natural causes, one of a drug overdose, and one of a fall from a balcony listed as an apparent suicide.

The reports of thugs killing cops and National Guardsmen were bogus, as were the tales of man-eating alligators. There were no substantiated reports of mobs firing on rescue helicopters. Nobody ever reported a baby being raped, a seven-year-old being murdered, a mob killing the man who killed the seven-year-old.

"The incidents were highly exaggerated," a Louisiana National Guard spokesman told the AP. "For the amount of people in the situation, it was a very stable environment."

So where did all these stories come from? And why were so many officials and mainstream news organizations so quick to repeat them?

As is the case with most widespread urban legends, a number of ingredients contributed to the mix.

First, the situation in New Orleans was beyond awful. The response to the disaster by state and federal authorities was scandalously, shamefully slow. People were dying in the streets. The conditions in the Convention Center and in the Superdome were primitive. There were some examples of criminal and unethical behavior. One could certainly fathom such a situation spinning violently out of control.

Part of the problem was the near-complete collapse of traditional communications systems in the city. It was virtually impossible to verify stories—and rather than proceed with caution, too many officials (including the mayor and the chief of police) and too many reporters chose to believe the worst.

Racial stereotypes also played a factor. Consider the controversy that occurred when one AP photo caption said a black man "walks through chest deep flood waters after looting a grocery store," while a similar photo of two white residents noted they were wading through waters "after finding bread and water from a local grocery store." The AP said that in the first case the photographer had actually witnessed the man going into the store and taking items— but does that mean we're to assume the white folks left money on the counter for the bread and water?

Regarding the reports of rampant, vicious crimes, New Orleans *Times-Picayune* editor Jim Amoss told the *Los Angeles Times*, "If the dome and Convention Center had harbored large numbers of middle-class white people, it would not have been a fertile ground for this kind of rumor-mongering."

Then there was the phony e-mail, supposedly from a doctor who volunteered at the Astrodome and claimed:

> Only one out of 10 people would say "Thank you." . . . They would ask for beer and liquor. . . . They treated us volunteers as if we were SLAVES. . . . I was laughed at and more "white boy jokes" were made at me. . . . I saw ONE white family and only TWO Hispanic families. The rest were blacks. Sorry, 20 to 30 percent decent blacks and 70 percent LOSERS . . . thugs and lifetime lazy-ass welfare recipients . . . like idiots we are serving the people who will soon steal our cars, rape, murder and destroy our city while stealing from our pockets on a daily basis through the welfare checks they take.

The e-mail was pure fiction, penned by someone with a small brain, a foul heart, and extremely limited communication skills. Still, it made the rounds, forwarded by people who, for whatever pathetic reasons, wanted to believe it was true.

Hurricane Katrina was a natural disaster greatly exacerbated by a lack of preparation, a city that ignored published warnings for years, incredibly inadequate early response from local and national leaders, and, in some cases, bad behavior on the part of a very small pocket of thugs and criminals. In reality, though, the great majority of Louisiana and Mississippi residents—even those who had lost loved ones and everything they owned—did not resort to lawlessness or shameful behavior. They struggled to survive and endure, they mourned their losses, and they helped one another in whatever ways they could.

That's the real and lasting headline about human behavior in the wake of Katrina.

7

THE VAST LEFT-WING CONSPIRACY

This is Fox News with the latest liberal outrage. It seems liberals want to give NASA the right to abort space missions whenever they feel like it!

—From a *Simpsons* episode lampooning
the Fox News Channel

Nearly every day I hear from a conservative who says he or she can't trust the mainstream press because "you're all liberals."

You know what? It's true. There really is a vast left-wing conspiracy to keep all conservatives quiet. We don't let them write for our newspapers, we won't let them go on TV, they have no voice on radio, and they'll never have a chance on the Internet.

But seeing as how we liberals control the media, I'm just trying to figure out why we're giving a voice to the likes of Rupert Murdoch, Sean Hannity, Bill O'Reilly, Matt Drudge, Rush Limbaugh, the *Wall Street Journal*, Fox News Channel, the *New York Post*, Cal Thomas, the *Washington Times*, the *American Spectator*, John McLaughlin, Ann Coulter, Glenn Beck, Bernard Goldberg, Cokie Roberts, Newsmax, George Will, Brit Hume, Michael Reagan, Robert Novak, Michael Kelly, Pat Buchanan, Steve Dunleavy, Michelle Malkin, the *New York Sun*, Michael Savage, Linda Chavez,

Kate O'Beirne, Oliver North, John Gibson, Tucker Carlson, William Kristol, Bill Bennett, Peggy Noonan, Charles Krauthammer, Andrew Sullivan, Joe Scarborough, Fred Barnes, Monica Crowley, the *Chicago Tribune*, Tony Blankley, Brent Bozell, David Limbaugh, Andrea Peyser, Dick Morris, Mona Charen, William F. Buckley Jr., Stephen Chapman, Laura Ingraham, Debbie Schlussel, Dennis Prager, the *Weekly Standard*, David Horowitz, John Stossel, and about 7,000 others. How'd they slip through?

We're *thisclose* to total domination!

III

SPORTS AND
GAMING

8

ONLINE POKER CONSPIRACIES FLUSHED OUT

This @$#! site is so rigged! They don't even try to make it seem fair. What a &!$@ joke.

—Losing player on the PokerStars Web site after suffering a "bad beat" in the Sunday Million tournament (the winning player in this particular hand was the author of this book)

I've been playing Texas Hold'em and other forms of poker as an amateur for about 10 years now. I've participated in events such as the World Series of Poker, the Heartland Poker Tour, and the Wynn Classic; I've played in tournaments at the Bellagio, the Venetian, Caesars, the Rio, and Mandalay Bay; I've taken part in dozens of charity events and in hundreds of amateur tournaments where we play for "funsies" only, because of course playing for real money would be illegal, ahem.

I've also played a few hands online, on sites such as the Mac-friendly Poker Room (which is now off-limits to U.S. players, since it declined to fight the restrictions of the Unlawful Internet Gambling Enforcement Act of 2006), and Full Tilt, PokerStars, and Ultimate Bet (all of which challenged the applicability of the UIGEA and continued to accept funds from U.S. players). Here you can risk real cash in games ranging from one-table tournaments to major events, with literally thousands of entrants and six-figure prize money.

From Australia to the Netherlands to Germany, from Hong Kong to Canada to the United States, there are people who make their living sitting at a computer for 8 or 10 hours a day, staring at virtual poker tables and wagering against opponents from all over the world.

Play at any one of those sites or just "visit" a game as an online lurker and it's only a matter of time before someone types one of the following messages in the chat box:

"This site is rigged!"

"These guys are such crooks!"

"What a scam, this game is fixed!"

"I'm never coming back here again. It's obvious they're rigging the games."

In nearly all of these cases, the person making these allegations has just suffered what is known as a "bad beat"—that is, losing a hand they were favored to win. (Sometimes they think they're favorites but they were actually underdogs in the hand, because they didn't understand the odds.) For example, if you're playing Texas Hold'em and you have a pair of Aces—the best possible starting hand—and you bet all your chips, and your bet is "called" by someone with a pair of sixes and you end up losing the hand, that's a basic bad beat. In another scenario, if you get to the final, "river" card on the board and there's only one possible card in the deck that can give your opponent the winning hand, and that one card that can defeat you comes up—well, that's a *really* bad beat.

Which leads to the most insincere congratulatory comment in the history of competitive gaming:

"Nice hand, sir."

"Nice hand" as in "You just got incredibly lucky."

"Sir" as in "asshole."

◎

Conspiracy theorists abound on the Internet poker chat boards, blathering endlessly about the various ways in which one can be cheated by other players and/or the sites themselves.

Just a few of the ways in which the game supposedly can be fixed:

- In tournaments, the sites arrange it so the "short stacks" (players with a relatively small number of chips) are knocked out as quickly as possible. Why? Because those players are likely to enter another tourney, which means they'll have to pay another entry fee to the site. (The sites make money by charging a percentage to each player entering a tournament. So if it's a $100 entry fee, you'll actually pay $110 to gain access to the tournament.)
- Online sites use "bots," or computer-generated players. How do you know the "person" sitting next to you at the table is really a person?
- Players at the same table can collude together by talking on the phone or deliberately dumping chips to one another.
- You'll see an excess of "premium hands" such as Ace-Ace, King-King, Ace-King, and Ace-Queen, in order to stimulate action and increase the chances that two or more players will go all-in on a particular hand. Once again, this would be done to get more players involved more quickly so they'll be eliminated and enter another tournament, thus giving the site yet another "rake fee."
- So-called "bad beats" occur far more often online than in real-world, "brick and mortar" tournaments. Further proof that it's all rigged!

"It's so rigged it ain't funny!" said one poster on a poker chat site.

> Why would [the online sites] want to have the big stacks favored in all matchups? Because it would get the losing short stack into another game quicker—cycle the players in and out of the games

as quickly as possible gets them more money! Something just isn't right. I'm going to withdraw my money and stick to land-based games!

When someone tried to explain that "poker is math" and under-dogs sometimes win, another conspiracy theorist chimed in:

You, sir, must be kidding yourself if you don't think Party Poker is rigged for what I call "Rake-a-romas." The table I was at last night had five flushes within the first 22 hands ... in short, there is no doubt the hands are rigged.... I saw AA versus KK three times last night ... how often does that happen in your home games? Do the math.

Of course, the player offered no proof of these unusual occurrences—but even if the hands played out just as he described, it would not be proof that a site was rigged. Anyone who has played any amount of poker, in person or online, can tell you about strange streaks when the cards run crazy. It doesn't mean anything.

In summer 2007, I played in a charity tournament at the World Series of Poker, hosted by Don Cheadle and featuring such celebrities as Ben Affleck, Matt Damon, Jason Alexander, Adam Sandler, Shannon Elizabeth, and Charles Barkley, as well as many of the world's top pros, including Phil Gordon, Daniel Negreanu, Doyle Brunson, Mike Matusow, and Phil Hellmuth.

At one point in the tournament, Cheadle got the extremely rare royal flush. Someone at my table said, "Yeah right, the host of the tournament just happens to get a royal flush." As if the dealer had stacked the deck to give Cheadle that hand.

Never mind that by the time the tournament reached the final table, virtually all of the celebrities and famous poker pros had been eliminated, even though a celeb-heavy final table would have made for a better story. (I was gone too.) For that brief moment when the host of the tournament was dealt the best hand imaginable, at least one player thought, "Conspiracy."

The odds against getting pocket Aces are 220 to 1—but that doesn't mean you're going to get pocket Aces exactly once every

220 hands. I played in a tournament in 2007 in which I found pocket Aces in my hand *four times* within about three hours.

Then I went about four hours without getting any pair even once. That's the way it goes.

Every major poker site has tracking devices in place to look for examples of "chip-dumping" among players or players using multiple identities to increase their chances of winning. However, there's probably nothing that can be done to prevent two players from entering a one-table "Sit and Go" tournament at the same time and talking with each other on the phone about their respective hands.

Not that this would guarantee results. You'd still be in the dark about the other seven players at the table. And if you and your buddy continually show up at the same table and the results look fishy, you might find yourselves banned from the site.

In fact, there *have* been some major cheating scandals in the online poker world in the last couple of years—but in every notable case, it's been players, and not the site operators, that were caught with their hands in the cookie jar.

In separate incidents, two online players were nailed for "multi-accounting"—in which a single player obtains multiple online identities so he or she can enter a one-entry-per-player tournament multiple times.

Another scandal occurred on the Absolute Poker site, where several players suspected another player of somehow being able to see his opponents' hole cards (which are supposed to be hidden from view). Apparently this player had obtained a "superuser" account that gave him access to this information. The owner of Absolute Poker's Web site released a statement acknowledging "a security breach in our system that allowed unlawful access to player information that resulted in unfair play. . . . It appears that the integrity of our poker system was compromised by a high-ranking trusted consultant employed by AP whose position gave him extraordinary access to certain security systems. . . . We will pay for all losses suffered by the affected players."

Then there was the controversy at PokerStars, the biggest online poker site in the world. The winner of the main event of the 2007 World Championship of Online Poker (WCOOP), a player named "TheV0id," was disqualified and had to forfeit a first-place prize of more than $1 million. Allegedly, it was another case of multi-accounting: a professional player reportedly set up TheV0id's account in his sister's name, and when the player was eliminated under his own name, he took over the spot registered to TheV0id. A number of other players noted that TheV0id had never played in any kind of tournament before—making it highly unlikely that he or she would best a field of several thousand to win such a high-stakes tournament. They reported their suspicions to PokerStars, an investigation was conducted—and the TheV0id was given the boot.

In every one of these cheating scandals, the sites acted quickly and decisively to correct the problem, disqualify the perpetrators, and issue refunds.

As for the more sweeping charges that the sites themselves fix the games: as always, we have to look at the pluses and minuses for such a conspiracy to exist.

On the plus side, if a site artificially sped up the games, it's possible it'd see an increase in tournament entry fees. On the other hand, if it seems as if the cards aren't coming straight and true and in random fashion, a site would risk losing players to other sites.

The major sites rake in millions of dollars in legitimate entry fees, with absolutely no risk. They're not gambling; they're charging you a fee to gamble. Why take a chance on losing their credibility, their license to operate, and their freedom from criminal prosecution by rigging the site? It's not even close to being worth the risk.

It's technically possible to enter bots in tournaments, but a bot playing poker would only know how to play the odds in a given hand. A skilled Internet player would probably welcome the chance to go heads-up against a robotically predictable opponent.

The conspiracy theorists among online poker players believe these gigantic sites are paying extremely close, computerized attention to *their* games. Even if they're playing for relatively low stakes, they're convinced the odds are artificially stacked against them.

They claim that when they first joined a particular site, they were given an excess of premium hands and lucky draws, the better to fuel their enthusiasm for playing on that site. They say that once they started winning "too much," the cards cooled off.

They'll tell you all about various bad beats when players made terrible calls, only to get lucky and "suck out."

Well, yes. To quote the cliche, that's poker.

There's no way to determine if sites provide extra doses of "beginner's luck" to new players, but there's also no proof of any such pattern. As for the losing streaks and bad beats—players always remember the bad luck stories more vividly than they remember the times when they were the lucky ones. It's human nature.

You see more bad beats online because there are far more hands dealt per hour in a computerized game than in a real-world game—and far more novice players who play hands they should be discarding. Online, you have jokers who will play literally any hand and bet like maniacs, because they're drunk, they're crazy, they don't care about their money, or they literally don't understand how the game is played.

One of the things even some of the whiny pros seem to forget about the game of poker is that not every hand will play out according to the expected odds. If that were the case, nobody would bother playing, because it would be the most boring and predictable game in the world.

9

THE NFL: NATIONAL FIXED-BALL LEAGUE

Blatant favoritism for a corrupt outcome . . . no more [purchasing] official NFL items for this family . . . the NFL should feel ashamed to have offered this sham to the nation and the world. Hope all the kickbacks and bribes were worth it, I'm done with you forever.

—Comments from the 19,862nd person to sign the "NFL Is Fixed" petition, started by a Seattle Seahawks fan after Super Bowl XL, which the Seahawks lost

Ask any pro football expert or diehard fan to select the most significant games in the history of the sport, and two contests will be mentioned again and again:

1. The 1958 NFL title match-up between the New York Giants and the Baltimore Colts at Yankee Stadium, won by the Giants in sudden-death overtime.
2. Super Bowl III, with "Broadway" Joe Namath and the upstart New York Jets of the American Football League defeating the heavily favored, old-school NFL champ the Colts, 16–7.

The Colts-Giants clash from December 28, 1958, is routinely cited as "the greatest game ever played," because it is widely considered to mark the birth of the modern, TV-friendly NFL. The nationally televised contest (except for a blackout in New York), featuring a total of 12 players and three coaches who would be inducted into the Hall of Fame, was an exciting and dramatic tug of war, with a half-dozen momentum-swinging turnovers, numerous clutch offensive plays, some great defensive stops, and a last-minute, game-tying drive that set up the first overtime in NFL championship history.

As the cliche goes, you couldn't have scripted a better game.

As the conspiracy theorist says: maybe that's exactly what happened.

Super Bowl III wasn't the most exciting or well-played game of the 1960s, but it's part of NFL lore as one of the monumental upsets in all of sports history—a victory that catapulted the rag-tag, beleaguered American Football League from something of a joke to near-equal status with the establishment NFL.

These two landmark games are forever linked because they changed the face of pro football forever. If the 1958 game established the NFL as a TV sport to be reckoned with, the 1969 game marked the true birth of the Super Bowl as the country's single biggest sporting event and football as the new national pastime.

Oh, and the games have one other thing in common.

They both were rigged.

Walk into any sports bar in any city in the United States on a football Sunday, wait for a call to go against the home team, and you're bound to hear it from some beefy guy in a modified mullet haircut, a genuine replica jersey barely containing his ballooning gut, and a giant basket of buffalo chicken wings in front of him.

"How can you make that $!%!& call, ref!!! Ah, this $&@! game is so #&!*! fixed it's a $#!&! joke!"

And then he'll order his 14th beer—a light beer, of course, because he's watching his weight.

If you ask that knowledgeable fan (who hasn't played the game since he was in fourth grade and doesn't know a single person who works for the NFL or for any of the television networks covering the NFL) for proof the game is fixed, he's likely to throw a half-eaten buffalo wing at you or shake his head at your naivete. If you don't understand how things work, he can't help you.

But come on, everybody knows the games are fixed.

Everybody knows "they" can get to the refs or to a couple of key players who will throw a game for the right amount of money.

Everybody knows the television networks and the NBA conspire to favor the major-market, glamorous teams, such as the Los Angeles Lakers and the Chicago Bulls and the New York Knicks and the Miami Heat.

Everybody knows the NFL takes care of certain favored players and teams.

Everybody knows the NBA draft lottery is a joke.

It's all fixed!

Let's take a look at the conspiracies swirling around those two landmark NFL games.

I've never heard anyone make the claim that the winning team of the 1958 NFL Championship Game was predetermined—but there are many who believe the final score was tainted.

The Baltimore Colts were favored by anywhere from 3½ to 5½ points over the New York Giants. According to the legend, Colts owner Carroll Rosenbloom, a colorful character and notorious high-stakes gambler, wagered a cool $1 million—worth about $7 million in 2007 dollars—on his team to cover the spread. (According to some versions of the story, Rosenbloom had a partner with whom he split the bet 50/50.)

At the end of regulation, the score was tied at 17—the first time in league history a championship game had been knotted up after four quarters. The concept of sudden death overtime was so foreign, even the players weren't sure what would happen next.

Colts quarterback Johnny Unitas, on NFL.com: "When the game ended in a tie, we were standing on the sidelines, waiting to see what came next. All of a sudden, the officials came over and said, 'Send the captain out. We're going to flip the coin to see who will receive.' That was the first we heard of the overtime period."

The Giants won the toss and took the ball, but they went three plays and out and had to punt.

Unitas and the Colts took over on their own 20-yard-line and proceeded to march down the field. When the Colts reached the 8-yard-line, they were in chip-shot field goal range—yet Unitas threw a supposedly dangerous pass to tight end Jim Mutscheller, who conveniently went out of bounds on the 1-yard-line.

"All I had to do was raise up and loft the ball to Mutscheller and make a hero out of him," Unitas told NFL.com. "But he decided to fall out of bounds at the one instead of going over the goal line. I guess it was slippery over there."

Hmmmmm.

Surely the Colts would kick the easy field goal now, right?

But wait. Let's not forget about that point spread. Whether Rosenbloom had the Colts giving away 3½ points or even 5½ points, a touchdown would be enough to cover the line, whereas a field goal would mean the Colts would win the game but Rosenbloom would lose the bet. (Ask any sports gambler about the agony of giving away 3½ points or more and watching "his" team settle for a chip-shot field goal instead of a touchdown, and he will have a story to tell you.) Legend has it that Rosenbloom called down to the sidelines and ordered Coach Weeb Ewbank—to this day the only man I've ever heard of who went by the name of "Weeb"—to eschew the field goal and go for the touchdown.

On the next play, Unitas handed off to Alan Ameche, who punched it in for the winning score. That gave the Colts a 23–17 victory—there was no need to kick the extra point—and gave Rosenbloom his million-dollar win.

Or so the story goes.

Many of the principals involved in the game and in the story—including Rosenbloom, Unitas, Ewbank, and Colts kicker Steve Myhra—are gone. Rosenbloom, who later owned the Los Angeles Rams, drowned in the ocean behind his Florida home in 1979—a death many found suspicious, given Rosenbloom's gambling habits and his alleged associations with shady characters, not to mention that he was an accomplished swimmer.

Stories about Rosenbloom's supposed $1 million bet and his command to Ewbank to go for the spread-beating touchdown began circulating almost immediately after the game, but nobody ever proved that the Colts owner actually ordered the coach and his players to eschew the field goal.

In Dan Moldea's 1989 book *Interference: How Organized Crime Influences Professional Football*, Unitas and Ewbank denied even knowing about the point spread.

"I called all the plays," said Unitas, a hero of the game and a man of impeccable reputation. "I was responsible for calling the pass [to Mutscheller] and for calling Ameche's number for the winning touchdown."

Moldea interviewed Ewbank, who said, "I was with the Colts for nine years, and I never talked to Carroll Rosenbloom or any of his friends during a ball game. I wasn't even conscious of what the line on the game was. Carroll never told me anything like that. He never gambled around me."

Guess it comes down to whether you want to believe the likes of Weeb Ewbank, a decent, player-friendly, straitlaced football lifer whose dedication to the game was such that his house was a veritable museum to college and professional football; and Johnny Unitas, the high-top-wearing, crew cut–sporting, preternaturally "square" quarterback—or if you'd rather put stock in unsubstantiated rumors that claim these two, among others, conspired to go for the TD rather than the field goal because they wanted their boss to win a bet. And no one ever felt enough remorse to go public?

Could it be that Ewbank and Unitas went for the touchdown because the field was torn up, making a snap-and-hold a riskier-than-normal proposition? Also, the Giants had blocked a Myhra field goal attempt in regulation, and Myhra had the second-worst field goal percentage in the league, making just 5 of 14 attempts that year. How about the fact that Ameche had fumbled only once all season? It could be argued that the handoff to Ameche was a safer play than a field goal attempt at that point.

Nobody is disputing that Rosenbloom was a high-stakes gambler. It might well be that he bet a huge sum on his team to cover the spread in the 1958 championship game—though a bet of $7 million in today's dollars would almost certainly have to be fanned out to a dozen or more bookmakers, since no single bookie would take that kind of action. And the more bookies involved, the more likely somebody would have blown the whistle on Rosenbloom. (One way to get out of paying out on a huge loss is to drop a dime on the winning bettor. He can't collect from you if he's in jail.) Then again, nobody has ever proved that Rosenbloom actually contacted Ewbank about the bet, either before or during the game, or that Ewbank and Unitas conspired to go for the touchdown in order to please the team owner.

In a chapter in a crazy-ass but undeniably entertaining book titled *The New Conspiracy Reader*, Brian Tuohy states:

> Over the years, there has been speculation about whether Super Bowls are "won," or whether they are "awarded." Some Super Bowls are awarded because of the stories they provide, others as rewards, but each for a reason: for instance, to Green Bay for bringing tradition back to the game; to Denver and John Elway in 1997 for their long-suffering seasons (perhaps at the League's insistence); to St. Louis and Tennessee in 1999 for their willingness to relocate for the League; to the relocated Baltimore Ravens in 2000 for their long-time owner, Art Modell, whose commitment

to the NFL reaches back to the 1960s; and . . . in perhaps one of the most blatant examples of scripting an entire season, to the 2001 New England Patriots. In an immediately post-9/11 America, what more symbolic team could the NFL crown its champion than the Patriots, who were the biggest underdog in Super Bowl's 36-year history?

Gee, I don't know. How about the *New York* Giants or the *New York* Jets? Wouldn't a Super Bowl champion from New York be a better story than a Super Bowl champion from New England? Are we supposed to believe that the entire 2001 season (including the opening weekend games, which took place prior to 9/11) was scripted to award the Super Bowl to a team *based on its nickname*?

You could take almost any Super Bowl and make the claim that the outcome was scripted in order to reward some beloved veteran player or some franchise owner for one reason or another. Every year, there are a half-dozen feel-good stories about the 15-year pro who finally wins the Super Bowl on the eve of his retirement, or the coach who maintains his focus even as his wife battles an illness, or the running back who has overcome a lifetime of smoking pot and hitting the strip clubs and has found Jesus just in time to carry the ball 23 times for 175 yards and the winning TD. And you know what? If those feel-good-story guys lost, there'd be some feel-good-story guys on the other team with equally compelling tales.

Tuohy correctly notes that Super Bowl III was a "turning point for the NFL," giving the AFL instant cred and paving the way for huge TV deals. But he veers into fantasyland when he suggests that Joe Namath guaranteed the Jets victory because the game was fixed.

"I would suggest Joe Namath is the 'smoking gun' of the NFL," writes Tuohy—and there are some women from the time who might agree with him, if Tuohy were talking about Joe's off-field prowess. But he's not, he's saying, "Super Bowl III was the first—but definitely not the last—time that the NFL fixed the outcome of one of its own games."

Tuohy then proceeds to offer absolutely no evidence that Super Bowl III or any other game was fixed, either by the players, the coaches, the referees, or the Budweiser Clydesdales. A typical example of his "evidence" is his mention of Super Bowl XXX, in which Pittsburgh's Neil O'Donnell threw two interceptions right into the arms of Cowboys defensive back Larry Brown.

"In the following off-season, both O'Donnell and Brown signed multi-million dollar free-agent contracts with other teams, going on to careers of mediocrity," writes Tuohy.

Uh-huh. And that proves . . . what, exactly? That O'Donnell and Brown were in on the fix for Super Bowl XXX and that the Jets (which signed O'Donnell) and the Raiders (the team that signed Brown) also were in on the conspiracy and gladly awarded lucrative contracts to these two?

After the Packers won the first two Super Bowls (which weren't even called Super Bowls at the time) by scores of 35–10 and 33–14, respectively, there was understandable skepticism about the quality of play in the AFL.

The Colts were huge favorites to stomp the Jets in Super Bowl III. Despite an early-season injury to the great Johnny Unitas, Baltimore had gone 13–1 in the regular season, dominating opponents with the league's second-best offense and the top-ranked defense. Some long-time observers were already calling the Colts one of the greatest teams of all time.

The New York Jets, coached by our old friend Weeb Ewbank, were 11–3 and had just squeezed past the Raiders in the AFL championship game. The Jets had a strong defense and a high-powered offense, but Namath was hardly a dominant quarterback in 1968. He had just 15 TD passes (as opposed to 17 interceptions) and had yet to become the "Broadway Joe" who would grow a Fu Manchu mustache, wear pantyhose for a TV commercial, star in movies such as *C.C. and Company*, and receive a Golden Globe nomination for New Star of the Year (Male) for his work in *Norwood*, and no, I'm not making that up.

Namath's famous Super Bowl "guarantee" wasn't a staged event. Responding to a heckler at the Touchdown Club three days before the big game, the brash young Namath shot back, "We're gonna win the game. I guarantee it."

If the fix was in, why would Namath make such a guarantee? Wouldn't it have made more sense for him to keep his mouth shut? Ah, but maybe he made the guarantee just so it wouldn't seem so suspicious, because after all why would he make the guarantee unless there was *no* fix, or so he wanted you to think?

Or something like that.

Thanks to a punishing ground game and some precision passing by Namath, the Jets defeated the Colts 16–7. It wasn't a fluke win. They were faster and stronger than the opposition, and they outplayed them from start to finish. And just like that, the AFL was no longer a joke.

Since then, a number of conspiracy theorists, including at least one participant in the game, wondered if the dramatic upset was just a little too convenient and too timely.

Writes a blogger who calls himself jesus2: "I'll cut the crap and get to the point. Unitas' life—and that of his family—[were] threatened. Unitas [was] in on the fix."

He goes on to cite a play in which "Unitas makes eye contact with [a] Jets' defender before THROWING THE BALL SQUARELY IN HIS HANDS/STOMACH FOR THE INTERCEPTION. . . ."

> The Congress of the United States of America and the FBI have an investigation to do . . . the people of the United States of America need to know just who it was that threatened the lives of two of the most decent men in sports history: Johnny Unitas and Earl Morrall.

Ah, so that explains it. Both quarterbacks for the Colts feared for their lives, so they threw the game.

(And let's not forget, Carroll Rosenbloom still owned the Colts in 1968. Some say he had another $1 million bet on this game—only this time he had bet *against* his own team.)

So not only was Unitas in on the great point-spread caper of 1958, but he also conspired to lose Super Bowl III? And here we all thought he was one of the most respected players the game has ever known. Turns out he was more corrupt than Moe Green.

Super Bowl III conspiracy theorists love to cite the words of Colts' defensive end Bubba Smith, who raised questions about the legitimacy of the game in a *Playboy* interview and in a short passage in his autobiography. Smith claimed (incorrectly) that the AFL-NFL realignment of 1970 wouldn't have been approved if the AFL didn't win at least one of the first four Super Bowls. He questioned Coach Don Shula's strategy and made vague references to an unnamed Miami cab driver who supposedly told him that Rosenbloom had made a huge bet against his own team. (And we all know that when it comes to getting the most reliable, irrefutable information available, one should ignore research and inside sources and go straight to the nearest cab driver.)

Does anyone believe Don Shula would deliberately try to lose a Super Bowl so his owner could win a big bet?

The AFL-NFL merger was endorsed by owners in both leagues and approved by Congress in 1966. Even if the Colts had whipped the Jets 73–0, the Super Bowl was hardly in danger. (In fact, the next year the AFL's Kansas City Chiefs whipped the NFL's Minnesota Vikings 23–7, giving the "inferior" league two championships out of the first four Super Bowls.)

And while there's no disputing the fact that the Jets' upset win turned Namath into a superstar, provided the AFL with a tremendous credibility boost, and increased fan interest in the game, the Super Bowl was already a phenomenon before the Jets spun the upset. The first three Super Bowls attracted Nielsen ratings in the mid- to high-30s and market shares of approximately 70 percent. There was absolutely no need to risk the megabright future of the NFL on some elaborate game-fixing scandal involving at least one team owner and the quarterbacks on both sides of the ball.

Besides, even if we're to believe the completely unfounded and morally objectionable charges that the Colts' quarterbacks deliberately lost the game, how does that account for the Jets offensive line pushing around the Colts' defensive front, including Bubba Smith, who had a subpar game? Were they all in on the fix as well?

Bubba Smith is the only participant in Super Bowl III who ever expressed any doubts about the legitimacy of the game—and even Smith later backed away from his statements and said he didn't believe the game was fixed.

"It couldn't happen," Smith said in an interview with the Associated Press in 1983. "I never said they fixed the game."

Of course, you know what happened. "They" got to Smith, too. Whoever "they" are.

Nearly 40 years later, the Pittsburgh Steelers defeated the Seattle Seahawks 21–10 in Super Bowl XL. As someone who placed a wager on the Seahawks +4 points, I was less than thrilled with a number of questionable calls that went against Seattle, including an offensive interference ruling that took away a touchdown in the first half and a holding call in the fourth quarter that negated a Seattle first down at the Pittsburgh 2-yard-line when the Seahawks were down by just 4 points.

No doubt about it, the refs sucked in Super Bowl XL, especially if you were a Seattle fan. It was one of the worst cases of officiating I've ever seen in a major championship contest in any sport. Even Seahawks coach Mike Holmgren, usually a pretty classy guy, couldn't resist taking a shot at the officials at a rally in Seattle the day after the game, when he said he didn't realize his team would be playing the Steelers *and* the officials.

But even as I was cursing the refs and lamenting my losing bet, I never seriously considered the idea that the game was rigged.

Rabid fans of the Seahawks saw it differently. Convinced his favorite team had been robbed, a fan created the "NFL Is Fixed" Web site and invited other Seahawks fans to sign his petition.

"We . . . will no longer stand by and allow our pure game to be corrupted by blatant bias," read the manifesto on the site. "Super Bowl XL was the culmination of the most poorly officiated playoff[s] ever. This is completely unacceptable and unfair to us fans who pay money to the NFL in merchandise and ticketing sales with the assumption that the product put on the field is by no means fixed."

Literally tens of thousands of fans "signed" the online petition, with many adding comments that elicited two reactions from me:

1. I weep for the future of the English language.
2. A lot of people are truly, deeply paranoid.

I'm going to have to clean up the grammar and spelling just so we get through this together. A sampling of comments:

I will never watch another NFL game.... Goodbye NFL.

"I felt that Super Bowl XL was fixed from the beginning ... Pittsburgh [Super Bowl] merchandise [was] being sold at the stadium ... numerous bad calls were made ... the better team didn't win, the favored team did."

The foul play in this Super Bowl was so obvious, the NFL would be derelict to not at least conduct an investigation.

Just appoint the Steelers champs next time. It's faster and cheaper.

Just wondering what the payout from Pittsburgh was to the refs.

That game was the biggest fix I've ever seen. The NFL should be embarrassed and a rematch should be played.

On and on it goes. Nobody offers even a shred of evidence that the NFL or anyone else paid the officials to favor the Steelers, nor does anyone even explain why a Pittsburgh victory would be more beneficial to the league than a Seattle win. (True, there was some sentiment for the popular Jerome Bettis to win a Super Bowl before he retired, but it could be argued that the Steelers already had four Super Bowl titles while the Seahawks had never even been in a championship game; what would be so bad about a championship in Seattle?)

What you get is a bunch of fans bitching because their team lost. Yes, there were some lousy calls, but does that mean all those Steelers fans are aware of the fix but don't care because their team won? If you're really a fan, wouldn't you be outraged by a game-fixing scandal even if your side was the beneficiary? Who wants a tainted championship?

When Cal Ripken Jr. hit a dramatic home run in his last All-Star game in 2001, some said it was just a little too much of a storybook moment.

"It was a Dale Earnhardt Jr. pitch," said *Newsweek*'s Howard Fineman, appearing on Don Imus's radio show.

Fineman was referencing yet another sports conspiracy theory: that Dale Earnhardt Jr.'s win on the track where his father had died was just a little too convenient.

With the Ripken home run, the thinking was that Chan Ho Park served up a cupcake so the beloved superstar could have a home run in his last All-Star game. But as baseball broadcaster Joe Buck pointed out in an article in *USA Today*, "Think of what you're accusing the other guy of. Park is the first Korean-born player in the All-Star game. He didn't wake up and think, 'I'll groove a pitch to Cal Ripken Jr. to make his night.' It's ludicrous to think he would give that kind of cooperation."

This is one of the problems with any sports conspiracy theory: the notion that a top athlete would sublimate his ego, his competitive fires, his legacy, and his morals, and deliberately let an opponent get the better of him. Even Pete Rose drew the line at betting against his team. As ethically bankrupt as Rose was, he couldn't bring himself to make managerial decisions against his own team.

It was 1985. The year of "the Conspiracy Draft," as veteran NBA reporter Sam Smith of the *Chicago Tribune* labeled it in a 2007 article.

According to the urban legend, in the first year of the NBA lottery, the NBA wanted to make sure the New York Knicks won the right to select Georgetown's Patrick Ewing.

At the time, eight unlabeled envelopes for the #1 pick represented the eight teams eligible for that pick. The envelopes would swirl about in a plastic globe, and Commissioner David Stern would reach in and extract one envelope at a time. Rumor has it that the Knicks' envelope had been stuck in a freezer overnight so that Stern could identify it by touch. Conspiracy theorists say that if you watch the video, you can see Stern hesitate for just a moment before he selects the first envelope—proof of, well, um, something.

To test the "Frozen Envelope" theory, I placed an envelope in my freezer overnight and then had an accomplice put it in a salad bowl with seven "unfrozen" envelopes as I looked the other way. Sure enough, it was easy to identify the frozen envelope. But just because it's possible doesn't mean it happened. Nor is there any evidence to back up the claims that the NBA lottery was rigged in 1993 so Orlando could get Penny Hardaway, rigged again in 1999 so the Chicago Bulls could get the #1 selection, and rigged yet again in 2001 so Michael Jordan's Washington Wizards could get the top pick.

(Not that having the #1 pick guarantees you're getting the best player anyway. Jordan and the Wizards selected Kwame Brown in 2001, while Gilbert Arenas fell all the way to the second round, becoming the 31st overall selection. Brown has career averages of about eight points and six rebounds per game. Arenas is one of the top scorers in the NBA.)

More than any other league, the NBA has been dogged by rumors about rigged drafts, fixed games, tainted All-Star balloting, you name it. If you were to believe all the conspiracy theories, the league is more corrupt than the Corleone family's "olive oil" business.

Among the theories:

- The Ping-Pong balls are weighted so certain teams can draft certain players.

- All-Star voting is rigged so the biggest names are assured of participating in the All-Star game, regardless of whether they're injured or having an off year.
- The refs make key calls that favor teams such as the Lakers, the Bulls, the Knicks, and the Suns, and players such as Kobe, Shaq, Dwayne Wade, and Steve Nash.
- The league conspires to make sure that playoff series go to six or seven games as often as possible, so the TV networks can make more money.

And you know why Michael Jordan retired the first time, right? He was getting into too much trouble with his gambling, so the league secretly suspended him and told him to say he was retiring, with the understanding that he would come back after a year or so.

Even some NBA players have openly questioned whether refs have made calls to ensure that playoff series go six or seven games. It's the last refuge of the whining loser.

The conspiracy theorists never address the most glaring flaw in all these game-fixing scenarios: the risk/reward factor.

Even if the NFL wanted to influence the outcomes of some games, why would "they" risk hundreds of millions of dollars in revenue, not to mention the credibility of the league and serious jail time, over one game?

It's no different in the NBA, which has been shadowed by rumors of game-fixing and draft-day shenanigans for decades. Are we really to believe that the league and officials conspire to favor certain teams such as the Lakers and the Knicks and the Bulls just because the ratings for those big-market teams will be somewhat higher? Then why do the Detroit Pistons and San Antonio Spurs keep winning championships?

The NBA has a six-year, $2.2 billion deal with TNT that runs from the 2002/2003 season until 2007/2008. It also has a six-year, $2.4 billion deal with ESPN/ABC. Would it make sense for the league to risk nearly *five billion dollars* in TV revenue just to extend a few playoff series and make a few million more in gate receipts and TV spots? If certain refs have been paid off, why hasn't anybody ever spilled the beans?

Listen to sports talk radio for any length of time or read the comments sections of many sports blogs, and you're bound to hear assertions that the NBA playoffs are rigged. Not only do the refs show favoritism to superstars such as LeBron James and major-market teams, but there's also a concerted effort to extend each series to as many games as possible, so the networks have more games (and more commercials) to showcase.

In summer 2007, the NBA was rocked by a gambling scandal when it was reported that veteran referee Tim Donaghy had allegedly wagered on a number of NBA games, including contests Donaghy had worked. Now the conspiracy theorists had legitimate ammunition for their arguments. Here was a guy who could directly influence the point spread by making foul calls (or looking the other way when violations were committed), and he was implicated in a major scandal.

However, nobody was saying the league itself or the TV networks were involved in the alleged corruption. In fact, the NBA cooperated with the FBI investigation—and behind closed doors, league officials were probably talking about how much they wanted to throttle Donaghy for messing with the goose that lays the golden eggs.

There have been game-fixing scandals in sports dating back to the 1919 "Black Sox." A few big names, including Paul Hornung, Alex Karras, and Pete Rose, have been involved in gambling scandals. Many others have been implicated but never formally charged with anything.

But the rumors about rigged Super Bowls or NBA drafts have never even graduated to plausible theory status, let alone concrete scandals. It simply makes no sense that the NFL or the NBA or Major League Baseball would risk billions of dollars in revenue and decades of building credibility in order to have a storybook upset or a "perfect" match-up.

Sometimes your favorite team loses. Sometimes the superstar gets favorable calls from the officials. Sometimes the refs blow it—and that usually means it was an honest mistake.

Usually.

10

CASINO CULTURE

[My friend] goes to Vegas at least twice a year, if only to visit his money. There, the casinos have no clocks, are open 24 hours, serve cheap booze and pump oxygen to keep gamblers awake.

—Article in the *Evening Times* of Glasgow (Scotland), February 5, 2007

It's all this money. This is the end result of all the bright lights and the comped trips, of all the champagne and free hotel suites, and all the broads and all the booze. It's all been arranged just for us to get your money. That's the truth about Las Vegas.

—Robert De Niro as Ace Rothstein in *Casino*

Trying to navigate your way through one of the megacasinos in Las Vegas makes you feel like you're trapped in the hedges in *The Shining. Didn't we just go this way? Are we going in circles? Which way is out? Is that the "Mamma Mia" ticket booth again? My God, we're trapped in the Wheel of Fortune slot banks and we're never getting out!*

Sure, there's signage everywhere indicating the way to the lobby or registration or the Sports Book or the Poker Room or the restaurants—but a lot of those arrows seem to be pointing at an angle that makes it almost impossible to discern which carpeted path one should take. I swear, some of these arrows point *up*, for crying out loud. Does that mean I'm supposed to flap my arms and fly to the all-you-can-eat buffet?

If you're trying to find your way out of the place, the task is even more arduous. They don't even provide signage paving the way to the exits. Why, it's almost as if they're trying to keep you on the gaming floor so you can lose more money!

Of course, that's exactly what "they" want to do.

Casino culture is a fascinating blend of romanticized mythology and mapped-out strategies, open-armed greetings and stone-cold intimidation, psychological trickery and hard math.

Every year, tens of millions of Americans flock to Las Vegas and Atlantic City—and riverboat casinos from Mississippi to Indiana to Georgia to Florida—knowing full well the deck is stacked against them in myriad ways. It's not exactly a conspiracy to separate you from your money, because they don't have to be that sneaky—but there are definitely some time-honored techniques employed by the casinos to stimulate action.

Las Vegas veterans love to regurgitate all the "facts" about what the casinos do to ensure you'll lose. Even if you've never been to Vegas, you've probably heard some of these stories—for example, there are never any clocks in a casino because they want you to lose all track of time.

Do the casinos ever cheat? It would be naive to think there's never been a case of a casino bending the rules, especially back in the days when the Outfit controlled the action. You can rig any game, from blackjack to roulette to the slots.

But here's the thing: why bother?

In most casino games, the house odds are almost criminally obscene anyway. Let's take a look at some of the most popular games and the percentages against you, the player:

Game	House Advantage
Baccarat	0.6 to 1.3%
Blackjack, single deck	0.2%
Blackjack, multiple deck	0.5 to 0.6%
Caribbean Stud Poker	5.2%
Craps, Pass/Come	1.4%
Craps, Any Craps	11%
Craps, Proposition 2, 12	13.9%
Keno	25 to 29%
Roulette	5.26%
Slots	4 to 16%

That's if you're playing optimum strategy. The house edge in blackjack is higher against players that don't double down when the cards are in their favor, stronger against craps players that don't take triple odds, etc.

We know this, and yet we gamble. We plan vacations, we buy plane tickets, we make hotel reservations, and we spend months looking forward to that weekend when we can go to Las Vegas, *where the odds are stacked against us.* The billionaires and the corporations put up the initial scratch, but we're the ones building those enormous, gleaming, 21st-century pyramids in the Nevada desert.

The casinos don't have to cheat at the games. All they have to do is keep you gambling—and to that end, there's an extremely deep reservoir of tactics they'll tap into, in order to ensure you spend as much time as possible gambling, or as we should more accurately call it, *losing.*

Casinos are like benevolent dictators. They'll shower you with comped rooms and free meals, they'll ply you with free drinks, they'll slap you on the back and ask if you're having a good time—

but if you start winning a bit too much, the smiles get a little cold, the inquiries a little intense.

A few years ago, I was a on a cruise ship that docked at Nassau, the Bahamas, for a day. I took the ferry to the Atlantis on Paradise Island, where I had stayed a half-dozen times in the past, and sat down at a blackjack table.

I got hot. Even though there's no mathematical justification for saying "I got hot," I got hot. Within about three hours, I had won several thousand dollars. It was time to get back to the ship, so I collected my chips and headed to the cashier's cage.

When I presented a cashier with a stack of high-value chips, she immediately asked for my room number. When I explained that I wasn't staying at the resort—that I had I stayed there in the past but was just visiting this time around—she called over a manager, who proceeded to quiz me as if I were on *60 Minutes*. Why wasn't I staying there? Would I like to spend the night? Which table was I playing at? How much was I playing per hand? Would I like to stay for dinner?

I finally grew impatient, identified myself as a member of the media, and asked if I could please have my cash without feeling as if I had somehow stolen it from them. They counted it out and handed it over, in businesslike fashion, and told me they'd love to see me again real soon.

Understand, I hadn't won enough to even put a dent in their profit for the week. They just didn't like the idea of someone coming in for a couple of hours and "taking" them for several grand before literally leaving the island.

Some blackjack hotshots have mastered the art of "card counting." (There are various levels of sophistication regarding this technique, but the basic act consists of keeping track of all the face-up cards and assigning a numeric value to each card. When there's a surplus of player-friendly 10s, face cards, and Aces remaining in play, you increase your bet accordingly.) In any casino, if they think you're counting cards at blackjack, they'll throw you out—even though card counting is perfectly legal. Remember, you're on private property, and it's not considered discriminatory to ban someone who is suspected of counting cards.

In the old days, if you were caught cheating or were even suspected of cheating, there was a good chance they'd take you in the back and physically discourage you from ever trying it again. (See *Casino*.) Today, it's more likely they'll throw you out and/or call the authorities—but not before they record and store your personal information so they can throw your ass out if you ever try to gain entrance again.

The Nevada Gaming Commission and State Gaming Control Board has a list of "Excluded Persons," most of them notorious for gambling-related offenses. For instance, "Douglas William Barr, Sr., is considered a career slot cheat who has shown no source of legitimate income for most of his adult life. He has been arrested over 150 times."

Of course, a good 99 percent of gamblers that enter casinos are neither card counters nor crooked cheaters. Like the customer who walks into an automobile dealership once every three to four years and thinks he or she can outmaneuver a 20-year veteran salesman who works the floor 10 hours a day, six days a week, the average gambler is overmatched from the get-go—and the casino stacks the odds even further through a mixture of technological, psychological, and architectural ploys designed to separate you from your money.

The Institute for the Study of Gambling and Commercial Gaming at the University of Nevada, Reno, publishes a phone book–sized tome titled *Designing Casinos to Dominate the Competition*, aka "the Book." It is crammed with analyses and tables and proven techniques in the areas of casino architecture, signage, decor, lighting, layout, etc.

Numerous design experts and scholars, such as Michael Shanks of Stanford, have studied the science and the psychology of casinos. When it comes to building a casino, nothing is left to accident. Everything from the placement of the tables to the pattern of the carpeting is planned with two things in mind—maximize the player count and keep the players playing.

Why are there no signs pointing you to the cashier's cage, which is inevitably tucked in the back of the casino? Because they don't want you visiting the cashier, of course.

Why do pit bosses sometimes offer show tickets or dinner coupons to gamblers who are riding a hot streak? Because they know you'll feel obligated to return to the tables after the show or the meal. After all, everybody was so nice to you.

When you sit down at a blackjack table and start with red $5 chips and green $25 chips, why do they insist on "coloring up" your chips when you leave, giving you black $100 chips? It's because a chip of any color just doesn't have the same visceral impact as a bill of a similar denomination. If you've got a pocketful of $100 chips, you're more likely to make your next bet a $100 bet.

Why does a craps table have oversized, brightly colored spots for long-shot wagers such as Hardways, Big 6, and Big 8, but only tiny signs tucked under the rail outlining the more favorable odds you can get on your number? Why is there no signage whatsoever behind the Pass line, where you actually place your chips to bet on those player-friendly odds? Why do you think?

On and on it goes. Where else but in a casino would you withdraw $500 from an ATM and receive five $100 bills? Why is it that the "suckers" at the bar have to pay $7 for a light beer but the gamblers at the tables or the slots get them for free, served up by cleavage-baring waitresses? Why is the entrance to most bathrooms at the far end of the casino while the exit from that same bathroom practically spits you right back onto the gaming floor?

These "tricks" are all perfectly legal. Let's take a look at some other casino techniques, real and imagined.

Claim: There are no clocks in casinos, and the dealers are prohibited from wearing watches.
Status: True and false.

You won't get the casinos to publicly acknowledge a ban on wall clocks—but I've been to virtually every major gaming establishment in Las Vegas, and I can't recall ever seeing a clock on the wall. There are more and more television sets in gaming areas—over the blackjack tables and roulette wheels, usually tuned to ESPN—and you might see an onscreen clock on the TVs, but not on the casino walls.

As for the no-watches policy, I've seen plenty of dealers that do wear watches. In fact, you can often catch a dealer sneaking a glimpse at a watch while dealing the cards, checking to see how long he or she has to listen to these vodka-guzzling putzes at the table before going on a break.

Claim: There are no windows in casinos.

Status: True—in most cases.

Most casinos still go with the old-school technique: no windows and smoked-glass doors, creating a perpetual nighttime atmosphere. But some of the newer establishments—for instance, the Wynn—incorporate natural light into their design.

Claim: They pump oxygen into the casinos to give you more energy and keep you awake.

Status: False. This is *the* enduring Vegas myth of all-time, repeated as fact in countless news articles and in millions of Vegas-related conversations. (It might have started with Mario Puzo's novel *Fools Die*, with the fictional Xanadu casino pumping in oxygen.) I was in Vegas in summer 2007, when temperatures hit 117 degrees, yet it was still so cool in the casinos that you had to wear a sweatshirt or long-sleeved shirt. There's no doubt the casinos keep the air chilly—but there's no mechanism pumping oxygen into the system.

Here's the thing about pumping oxygen into a room: any small fire could become a major problem because of the increased flammability of the air.

Claim: The slot machines are amplified so that when someone hits a jackpot, the sound reverberates.

Status: True. Even though in nearly all cases these days, the coins don't actually fall into the metal bins anymore—you push a button and a coupon is printed out—when someone wins, the clanging and banging sounds are loud enough to turn heads, whereas there's nothing but silence when a slots player taps out. On one popular slots game, an excited voice cries, "You're a winner!" But when you draw a blank, it's not as if the machine lights up and the mechanized voice says, "You're out of money! You're a *loser!*"

Claim: If you watch a slot machine and it's playing "cold," wait until the player gives up and then jump on that machine, since it's due to win.

Status: False. Veteran slots players will zealously guard "their" machines and will tell you about all sorts of formulas they have for beating the slots. Right—and if they're so successful, why are they wearing those bad clothes while playing the quarter slots? There's a reason why slot machines continue to take up more space—and more prominent space—on casino floors, compared with the space provided to table games. The reason is, the house has a much bigger advantage with slots.

The machines are calibrated to offer random odds. They don't have memories, they don't have "rhythms," and they don't "reset" if they yield a jackpot.

Claim: Thanks to all those cameras in the ceiling, the casino can decide who wins the next big jackpot.

Status: False. Even though the casinos can watch every move on the floor, each slot machine is controlled by a random number generator within the machine itself. Tampering with these computer chips is a felony, and the slots are regularly tested, at random, by independent experts.

In order to rig a floor filled with slot machines, a casino would have to hack each individual machine, pay off the inspectors, and hope that everyone involved keeps quiet about the conspiracy. But since the casinos already have a substantial advantage over slot players that's perfectly legal and hassle-free, why would they bother?

Claim: "What happens in Vegas stays in Vegas."

Status: False. What happens in Vegas winds up on your credit card statement.

11

CURT SCHILLING AND THE BLOODY RED SOX

I couldn't give two [bleeps] about what was on the sock, I care that we won the game.

—Red Sox general manager Theo Epstein, in an e-mail to the *Boston Globe*, April 2007

One of my favorite baseball movies of all time is *The Natural*. Even though director Barry Levinson created an ending that was a 180-degree turn from the dark finish of Bernard Malamud's brilliant novel, the cinematic version of the story stands alone as one of the great mythic celebrations of America's game.

Robert Redford, who had played ball up to the collegiate level, was perfectly cast as the mysterious, sweet-swinging Roy Hobbs. Unlike the stiff Gary Cooper in *Pride of the Yankees* or the noodle-armed Tony Perkins (God help us) in *Fear Strikes Out*, Redford actually looked like he belonged on a baseball field. He had a fluid throwing motion and a smooth swing.

Every time I see *The Natural*—and I watched it again recently thanks to a 2007 DVD version with restored footage—I get goose bumps at the ending, when Roy hits that mammoth home run that crashes into the light towers and sends sparks showering down like fireworks. It's classic.

But there's a moment just before Roy hits the home run that's inadvertently funny. It's the blood-on-the-jersey moment.

As you might recall, Hobbs had been poisoned by the duplicitous Memo (Kim Basinger), leaving him with some sort of internal bleeding in the abdominal area. He's laid up in the hospital and he almost dies, but he rallies just in time for the big game.

Cut to that final at-bat with the game on the line. With Roy down to his final strike, the opposing catcher shoots a glance at him and notices three bright red streaks of blood on Roy's jersey. Our hero is bleeding!

Huh?

Roy wasn't stabbed. (He had been shot, but that was about 15 years earlier. It's doubtful the wound just suddenly reopened.) How does an intestinal problem like that lead to an open wound? Was Roy's midsection about to explode like something out of *Alien*?

Chalk it up to poetic license. The point was that the greatest player who ever lived was finally getting a second chance, and he almost lost that chance. Roy's game-winning home run was all the more heroic because we knew he was in severe, crippling pain. Why, there was even blood on his jersey.

Fast-forward to the legendary 2004 American League Championship Series between the New York Yankees and the Boston Red Sox—the most vaunted rivalry in all of sports. (We know it's the most vaunted rivalry in all of sports because virtually every time the Yankees and Red Sox play, it's on national TV. According to the unconfirmed rumors, some ESPN executives believe the Chicago White Sox are the westernmost team in the American League.)

The Red Sox were attempting to do what no team had ever done in baseball history—come back from a three-games-to-none deficit in a postseason series. Red Sox ace Curt Schilling was set to take the mound for Game 6, but Schilling was in bad shape, suffering from an excruciatingly painful displaced tendon. Surgery was inevitable, but doctors agreed to temporarily suture the area so his ankle wouldn't pop out.

With the Fenway Park crowd roaring, Schilling turned in one of the grittiest pitching performances anyone had ever seen. Inning after inning, he kept the Yankee bats quiet, despite the excruciating pain. Close-up shots on TV revealed bright red blood soaking through Schilling's sock—like something out of *The Natural*—but he just kept going, pitching seven innings and yielding just one run on four hits.

"I don't think any of us have any idea what he went through to pitch tonight," said Red Sox manager Terry Francona in the postgame press conference. "For him to go out there and do what he did, his heart is so big."

The Red Sox won Game 6 by a 4–2 count, finished off the Yankees in Game 7, and went on to the win the World Series—in the process finally giving some peace and joy to all those hardcore Red Sox fans who drove the rest of the nation crazy with their "We're cursed" obsession. Schilling pitched Game 2 of the World Series, and the blood-soaked sock from *that* game was sent to Cooperstown, New York, for display in the Hall of Fame.

End of fairy tale—until spring 2007.

On an April night in Baltimore, Schilling once again went seven innings and allowed just one run as the Red Sox defeated the Orioles, 6–1. It was a relatively quiet game in the early part of the season and would have been quickly forgotten, if not for an offhand comment by Orioles announcer Gary Thorne during an exchange in the fifth inning with color man and Hall of Fame pitcher Jim Palmer.

"The great story we were talking about the other night was the famous red stocking [Schilling] wore when they finally won, the blood on his stocking," said Thorne, filling time as the game unfolded.

"Nah. It was painted," he continued. "Doug Mirabelli confessed up to it after. It was all for PR. Two ball, two strike count . . ."

According to the *Boston Globe*, Thorne said that veteran Red Sox catcher Mirabelli had told him about the bloody sock hoax a couple of years earlier.

When Mirabelli was told what Thorne had said during the game, he was livid.

"What? Are you kidding me? He's fucking lying," said Mirabelli. "A straight lie. I never said that. I know it was blood. Everybody knows it was blood."

Just like that, we had an instant conspiracy theory! The Internet was buzzing with debate, and callers to sports talk shows weighed in with their theories.

Not that this was the first time someone had questioned the authenticity of the bloody sock. During the 2004 World Series, the *Baltimore Sun* writer Laura Vecsey wrote:

> Now that Curt Schilling's postseason apparently is over after last night's start, maybe we can reflect on what is certain to become a legendary October performance.
>
> Some of us have been fixated on one distinct possibility: What if it wasn't blood on his sock during his Game 6 performance in the American League Championship Series?
>
> Maybe it wasn't blood. Maybe it was antiseptic or a few errant drops of anesthetic we saw. Does blood stay bright red through seven innings, exposed to air? Does blood come out of an area that, from distant observation of Schilling's naked foot, doesn't seem to be irritated to that degree, despite the sutures holding the tendon in place?

Vecsey quotes the Red Sox director of public information, who says, "It could have a little blood mixed in there." She notes that Schilling himself said it "might" have been blood.

"Call it embellishment," wrote Vecsey. "Call it poetic license. Call it a great sportsman amplifying his own legend."

Although Vecsey raised some interesting points, there was virtually no follow-up. The Red Sox completed the sweep of the Cardinals in the World Series, and the legend of the bloody sock became a permanent part of "Bah-ston" lore.

The rumor surfaced again in the February 2006 issue of *Gentleman's Quarterly* magazine, in a feature titled "10 Most Hated

Athletes in Sports." Schilling was ranked #4, with *GQ* commenting, "Some of his peers raise doubts about the famous bloody sock."

An anonymous "ex-teammate" is quoted: "All around baseball, people questioned that. It was funny how the stain didn't spread."

Again, though, the conspiracy theory never rose above the level of a whisper—until Thorne's comments in April 2007.

Thorne quickly backpedaled from the story, saying he had misunderstood what Mirabelli meant when the catcher had told him, "We got a lot of publicity out of that," meaning the bloody sock story.

Doug Mientkiewicz, a Yankee in 2007 but a Red Sox in 2004, said, "In my mind, it is a 100 percent falsehood that it was ketchup or paint or nail polish or whatever they said." The Red Sox team doctor at the time confirmed there was bleeding when the sutures were put in.

There's also the question of *why* Schilling would attempt such a con job, when he should have been concentrating on one of the most important games of his baseball life. Are we to believe that he thought he would gain a psychological advantage, or that he was so obsessed with building his own legend that he'd take the time and effort to paint his sock blood red?

Oddly though, it seemed as if a lot of people *wanted* to believe that Schilling had painted the sock red or that some other substance had caused the stain. Schilling's one of the least popular players in baseball; as one Red Sox reporter noted early in the 2007 season, 24 members of the team all agreed on one thing: Schilling should just shut up and pitch.

Fat chance.

With Thorne's comments creating a mini-firestorm in the baseball world, Schilling took to his own blog to offer a passionate, rambling rebuttal.

"Watching [ESPN personalities] Woody Paige or the plastered, made-up face of Jay Mariotti spew absolutely nothing of merit on sports, day after day, makes it easy to understand how Gary Thorne could say something as stupid, ignorant and uninformed as he did the other night," wrote Schilling, who goes on to praise Thorne as an "awesome" hockey announcer but notes they'd never met.

It was blood. You can choose to believe whatever you need to, but facts are facts. The 25 guys that were in that locker room, the coaches, they all know it....

Gary Thorne overheard something and then misinterpreted what he overheard. Not only did he misreport it, he misinterpreted what he misreported.

If you have nuts, or the guts, grab an orthopedic surgeon, have them suture your ankle skin down to the tissue covering the bone in your ankle joint, then walk around for four hours. After that, go find a mound, throw a hundred or so pitches, run over, cover first a few times. When you're done check that ankle and see if it bleeds.

All right, but if I follow that plan, it's going to take a while. I'll have to get back to you.

Schilling offered to donate $1 million to charity to anyone who could prove there was anything but blood on the bloody sock—but as he acknowledged in his blog, nobody knows where the sock is.

"I'm still convinced that the sock from Game 6 of the ALCS is [in the home of] someone that works in the Yankees' clubhouse," he wrote.

Really? If so, wouldn't you think that person would have stepped forward at some point to offer the sock to Schilling or Major League Baseball for a price? It's not like having a stolen Picasso at home that you can enjoy or show off to a few select friends. What's the point of having a dirty bloody sock, even the most famous bloody sock this side of O.J.'s place, if you can't get any money for it?

As for the World Series sock, a spokesman for the Baseball Hall of Fame told the *Boston Globe*, "Three years later, the blood stain that was once red is now a hue of brown, which is what happens to blood over time."

Odds are if the infamous bloody sock hasn't surfaced by now, it's gone forever. We'll never know for sure if Schilling doctored the sock or if some substance other than blood caused the bright red stain. What we do know is that just like Roy Hobbs, Curt Schilling came through with the game of his life as he endured pain that would put most men on their backs.

IV

ENTERTAINMENT

12

THE SOPRANOS' LAST SUPPER

The line to cancel HBO starts here. What a ridiculously disappointing end lacking in creativity. . . . There's even buzz that the real ending will be available only on the series' final DVD. Either way, it was terrible. . . . Chase clearly didn't give a damn about his fans. Instead, he crapped in their faces. This is why America hates Hollywood.

—*Deadline Hollywood* writer Nikki Finke, on the series finale of *The Sopranos*

The ending to *The Sopranos* was arguably the most controversial series finale since *Who's the Boss?*

For the record: I thought it was brilliant. Fans who wanted to see Tony get whacked or enter the witness protection program, fans who wanted to see Tony kill Paulie, fans who wanted some kind of big shoot-out or "twist" ending—what show were they watching all those years?

Of course *The Sopranos* had some stunning plot developments over the years, with major characters getting killed off in the blink of an eye. But it was never a prime-time soap opera, and it was never a twist-and-turn jigsaw puzzle like *Heroes*, for crying out loud.

If one of those vaguely menacing characters in the diner had pulled out a gun and we had seen Tony, Carmela, A.J., and maybe even Meadow laid out in pools of blood, you're telling me *that* would have been a great ending?

Come on. That's B-movie stuff.

The fact that people were still dissecting and arguing about *The Sopranos* in the days and weeks after the show ended says much about the genius of series creator David Chase, who made the decision to end the run on a somewhat ambiguous note. (It's not as if nothing happened in the last few weeks of Tony Soprano's life leading up to that family dinner. Most of his closest associates were either dead, in a coma, or, in the case of Uncle Junior, living in the Twilight Zone.) Five minutes after most series draw to a close, people stop talking about those shows. *JAG* ran for 10 years, but when was the last time you heard anyone talk about the series finale of *JAG*? Ever?

When a series finale packs in all big-ticket items such as weddings, births, deaths, resolutions of long-time conflicts, the closing of the business where everyone worked, etc., it feels rushed and gimmicky. Everyone on *Friends* finds love and/or happiness; the gang on *Seinfeld* gets sent to jail; Bob Newhart's second life was only a dream; the entire run of *St. Elsewhere* took place in the mind of an autistic kid—give me a friggin' break.

So what exactly *did* happen in the last moments of *The Sopranos*? That's where all the conspiracy theories kick in.

There were literally hundreds of *Sopranos* final episode conspiracy theories put forth on the Internet. Perhaps the two most well-known are the infamous "Nikki Leotardo" e-mail and an incredibly detailed analysis written by a former TV writer who began his fascinating essay with, "OK, here's 3000 words about five minutes of TV. I must have no life whatsoever."

In the days after *The Sopranos* finale, I must have received the Nikki Leotardo e-mail 100 times. Usually the subject header said something like, "THE SOPRANOS—YOU HAVE TO READ THIS!!!!!"

An excerpt:

> In the last scene we are seeing through Tony's eyes. Remember when he was speaking with Bobby, basically saying you don't see it happening [when you're killed]?
>
> So here is what I found out. The guy at the bar is also credited as Nikki Leotardo. The same actor played him in the first part of Season 6 during a brief sitdown concerning the future of Vito. Apparently he is the nephew of Phil. Phil's brother Nikki Senior was killed in a 1976 car accident. Absolutely genius!!! David Chase is truly rewarding the true fans who pay attention to detail.
>
> The trucker was the brother of the guy who was robbed by Christopher in Season 2. Remember the DVD players? The trucker had to identify the body.
>
> The Boy Scouts were in the train store.
>
> The black guys were the ones that tried to kill Tony and only clipped him in the car.
>
> Thank you David Chase for making it so obscure. I feel bad about hating you at first. Absolutely amazing!!!

If this had been a deleted scene from the movie *Crash* or it had been inspired by a flashback in *Lost*, maybe half the customers in the diner would have had some connection to Tony Soprano.

Problem is, not one of the assertions made in the e-mail is true.

The guy at the bar was not credited as "Nikki Leotardo." There never was a Nikki Leotardo on the show.

The Boy Scouts in the diner are not the same kids who were in the store when Bobby got whacked.

The actor playing the trucker had never been on the show before.

The two black guys in the diner were not the same two guys who tried to kill Tony. How do we know? Well, at least one of the two would-be assassins was killed when the attempt was botched.

However, the e-mail did get one thing right: the name of the show *is The Sopranos*.

Probably the most comprehensive and captivating dissection of the final scene was written by Bob Harris, author of a book about his experiences on *Jeopardy!* and a former writer on *CSI: Crime Scene Investigation*, among many other credits.

Harris penned a lengthy, labyrinthine, and well-crafted essay about the final scene in *The Sopranos* and posted it on his blog, where it soon became a huge Internet hit. I received at least a dozen e-mails directing me to his site.

In meticulous detail, Harris notes myriad examples of symbolism run amok in the final episodes. He points out that in the opening moments of the episode, Tony is filmed from above, making it appear as if he's lying in a coffin; he explains why the color orange is a direct reference to *The Godfather*; how Tony Soprano is framed in a *Last Supper* motif in one shot in the diner; how Tony, Carm, and A.J. gobble their onion rings as if they were communion wafers; and much, much, more. (You can read the entire essay at www .bobharris.com/content/view/1406/.) Harris makes some keen points and takes some wild leaps of faith, but as interesting as the essay is, it doesn't "prove" that Tony was killed or that he's still alive.

Other bloggers compiled lists of the music selections on the tabletop jukebox. Before Tony settles on "Don't Stop Believin'" by Journey, he flips past a number of selections that seem to have added significance, including:

- "Those Were the Days"
- "This Magic Moment"
- "Who Will You Run To?"
- "Magic Man"
- "I've Gotta Be Me"/"A Lonely Place"

Then there's the *Washington Post* article noting all the biblical references in the final episode. And the theory that the ubiquitous cat is the spirit of Adriana, reincarnated—which explains why the cat was fixated on the picture of Christopher, who gave up Adriana to be whacked. Not to mention the significance of the *Twilight Zone* episode playing on the TV in one scene. And the comments of a tour guide about how Little Italy is vanishing. And so much more.

David Chase commented cryptically to the *Newark Star-Ledger*, "Anybody who wants to watch it, it's all there." In an interview for *The Sopranos: The Complete Book*, he elaborated: "If people want to sit there figuring this stuff out, I think that's just great." But "there are no esoteric clues in there. No *Da Vinci Code.* . . . I'm not trying to be coy. It's just that I think to explain it would diminish it."

In the same interview, he marveled, "We didn't expect [some fans] to be *that* pissed for that long. . . . There *was* a war going on that week and attempted terror attacks in London. But these people were talking about onion rings."

There are more theories about the last episode of *The Sopranos* than about any series finale in the history of television. Some say Chase will one day do a movie version of *The Sopranos*; I say you'd have a better chance of getting James Gandolfini to play the mom in a Broadway revival of *Hairspray*. We'll never know exactly what happened after the screen went gray, because we're not supposed to know. Maybe Tony got whacked. Maybe Meadow joined the family for an uneventful dinner. Maybe 10 years past that moment in the diner, Tony would be in prison, Carmela would be divorced from him and married to someone else, Meadow would be an attorney representing shady clients, and A.J. would be in Hollywood, working as a producer and snorting his way to self-destruction.

Or maybe they'd be back in the diner for another meal, still a happy (if highly dysfunctional) family.

13

THE SECRET OF
THE SECRET

You can have, do, or be anything you want.

—From the trailer for the DVD of *The Secret*

Oprah Winfrey has been doing her talk show from Chicago for about as long as I've been working in the media in the city—and from time to time I've been the "Yeah, but . . ." in her life, writing columns that try to look at her exploits with a bit of restraint and common sense.

1988: Oprah loses 67 pounds and credits a weight-loss program. She sports a pair of size 10 jeans on her show while pulling a red wagon containing 67 pounds of fat.

Me: Yeah, but she did it through one of those dangerous liquid diets.

Epilogue: Two years later, Oprah has regained all that weight and then some. She warns her viewers about the perils of liquid diets.

1994: Oprah touts *In the Kitchen with Rosie: Oprah's Favorite Recipes*, which rises to the top of the bestseller lists and becomes one of the most popular books of the decade.

Me: Yeah, but the recipes are complicated and expensive and time-consuming to make (the ingredients necessary to cook one dish—paella for four—would have cost $75 at the time). Do Oprah's working-class fans have the money, time, and inclination to cook such exquisite dishes on a regular basis, or will the cookbook gather dust on shelves?

Epilogue: Bragging about the book reaching 6 million in sales, Oprah says, "Everybody has it. Nobody's cooked anything, but everybody has it." Apparently she feels no guilt over having millions of her fans pay $15 a pop for a cookbook they'll never use.

1998: Oprah gets increasingly spiritual on her show. The creepy "Venus/Mars" psychobabbler John Gray gets a regular segment. Another regular feature is called "Remembering Your Spirit." Oprah claims to hear the voices of slaves, says she has given them names, and says she has come to know each of them personally.

Me: Yeah, but this is kinda silly, isn't it? I label the talk show queen "Deepak Oprah."

Epilogue: In a speech in Washington, D.C., Oprah singles out my columns and says my newspaper doesn't understand what she's doing.

2000: Oprah's ego has ballooned to frightening proportions. The first edition of O, the Oprah Magazine has 14 pictures of Oprah. The second edition has an even dozen. Oprah conducts "Personal Growth Summits" in large arenas, at which she says things like, "Phenomenally, phenomenal woman—that's me." She tells a story of a woman who buys a pair of Oprah's used shoes at a charity auction. "To make herself better she would stand in my shoes," says Oprah.

Me: Yeah, but doesn't it bother Oprah that people are treating her like a religious figure?

Epilogue: Still waiting for my complimentary subscription to O.

2004: Oprah sends the studio audience into a greed-fueled frenzy when she announces that each and every one of them will be receiving a new Pontiac G6 sedan.

Me: Yeah, but Oprah didn't actually give away the cars—
Pontiac did, which means Oprah basically did an infomercial for
Pontiac. Also, while it was noted in nearly every mainstream news
story that "Pontiac will pay for the taxes and customizing of the
cars," the reality is that Pontiac was picking up the *sales* tax, not the
state and federal income tax. The lucky winners were responsible for
paying thousands of dollars in taxes—up to $7,000 in some cases.

Epilogue: A few of the winners said they'd have to sell their cars
immediately. Neither Oprah nor Pontiac offered to make up the tax
difference to the lucky winners.

I guess you can see why Roger Ebert was invited to Oprah's 50th
birthday party and I wasn't.

◎

Over the years, I've also praised Oprah in a number of columns—
for example, when she raked James Frey over the coals after learn-
ing his memoir (which previously she had praised to the skies on
her program) was filled with fabrications. Turns out that about
750,000 of the *Million Little Pieces* were figments of the author's
imagination.

But it could be argued that after the Frey debacle, Winfrey
touted a book that was even more problematic, and filled with
much more insidious nonsense. The ideas and philosophies spouted
in this particular book are ludicrous, insulting, and potentially
dangerous.

I speak of perhaps the most dominant book/DVD phenomenon of the first few years of the 21st century:

The Secret.

◎

Unless you know about *The Secret*, you are among the billions of
people who have been kept in the dark by the greatest and most
complete conspiracy since the beginning of time.

"The leaders in the past who had The Secret wanted to keep the power and not share the power," writes Dr. Denis Waitley, a psychologist and "trainer in the field of mind potential," in the introduction to the bestselling book.

"They kept people ignorant of The Secret. People went to work, they did their job, they came home. They were on a treadmill with no power, because The Secret was kept to a few."

According to Waitley and the other peddlers of *The Secret*, great leaders throughout history have had knowledge of a certain mindset that enabled them to achieve whatever they wanted. This secret was locked away for years—but now it's out in the open again, available to anyone who buys the book or the DVD, or hey, why not both?

"People have used The Secret to manifest their perfect homes, life partners, cars, jobs, and promotions, with many accounts of businesses being transformed within days of applying The Secret," writes Rhonda Byrne in the book's foreword. "There have been heart-warming stories of stressed relationships involving children being restored to harmony. Some of the most magnificent stories we have received have come from children using The Secret to attract what they want, including high grades and friends."

Contributor Bob Proctor elaborates on how deep the conspiracy runs: "Why do you think that 1 percent of the population earns around 96 percent of all the money that's being earned? Do you think that's an accident? It's designed that way. They understand something. They understand The Secret, and now you are being introduced to The Secret."

According to the teachings of The Secret, great leaders, including Plato, Shakespeare, Newton, Lincoln, Edison, and Einstein, all knew of The Secret—but it took Rhonda Byrne, Bob Proctor, Denis Waitley, and a host of other life coaches and motivational speakers and self-help authors to finally unlock the keys to The Secret and share them with us, the unenlightened masses. (I guess that means Byrne et al. are greater humanitarians than those selfish historical icons who kept The Secret to themselves all these years. I always knew Lincoln was overrated as a humanitarian.)

I read *The Secret*, and I have to admit it was very effective on one level: it gave me a decent workout because I had to keep getting up and retrieving the book after hurling it across the room in disgust.

Rhonda Byrne and her army of associates and disciples would have you believe there's a conspiracy of smart, enlightened people in the world who have long held access to the great solution of success in life—and you, too, can possess this "inside knowledge" if you just buy the crap she's peddling.

What's amazing to me is that Ellen DeGeneres, Larry King, Oprah, Montel Williams, and other opinion shapers have embraced this book when they should be denouncing it as immoral, unethical, and spiritually bankrupt.

Byrne's entire philosophy is based on "the law of attraction," which states that if you fully dedicate your thoughts and dreams and wishes to achieving something, the universe will act in accordance with your thoughts and make these things happen.

Here's how Byrne described it in an e-mail to the Associated Press:

"The law of attraction says that like attracts like, and when you think and feel what you want to attract on the inside, the law will use people, circumstances and events to magnetize what you want to you, and magnetize you to it."

Hence the term *chick magnet*.

Like a lot of people who have made it, Byrne falls into the trap of believing she made it primarily because she had big dreams and more than anything she wanted those dreams to come true. You get this every year at Oscar time, when some genetically gifted, talented, and extremely fortunate person says, "This proves that if you want something bad enough and you never let your dream die, you can make it all the way to the top! If you don't stop dreaming, it will happen to you!"

Maybe. Probably not. There are millions upon millions of people who work hard and wish hard and dream hard—just as hard as the superstars of the world—and never become rich or famous or even financially comfortable and respected by their peers. Winners of the life lottery often make the mistake of thinking they tapped into a special kind of belief system that made their dreams come true, when in reality it was probably a mix of hard work, God-given talent, and being in the right place at the right time.

According to author and "personal empowerment advocate" Lisa Nichols, one of the inside secrets of The Secret is understanding that "the law of attraction doesn't compute 'don't' or 'not' or 'no,' or any other words of negation."

> As you speak words of negation, this is what the law of attraction is receiving:
>
> "I don't want to spill something on this outfit."
> *"I want to spill something on this outfit and I want to spill more things."*
>
> "I don't want a bad haircut."
> *"I want bad haircuts."*
>
> "I don't want to be delayed."
> *"I want delays."*
>
> "I don't want to catch the flu."
> *"I want to catch the flu and to catch more things."*

So on one level the law of attraction can grant your every wish—but on another level, the law of attraction is apparently dumber than a puppy. You have to spell things out in a specific, nonnegative way, or the universe won't respond.

Here's an idea. Most people who say, "I don't want a bad haircut" actually don't want a bad haircut, unless they were in certain 1980s power metal bands.

Byrne's load of horseshit includes the claim that overweight people need only to think the right thoughts and they'll be thin.

"The first thing to know is that if you focus on losing weight, you will attract back having to lose more weight, so get 'having to lose weight' out of your mind," writes Byrne. If that makes sense to you I'll bet you can also bend spoons at will.

"The condition of being overweight was created through your thought to it," she writes. "To put it in the most basic terms, if someone is overweight, it came from thinking 'fat thoughts,' whether that person was aware of it or not. A person cannot think 'thin thoughts' and be fat. It completely defies the law of attraction."

Okay, let's put aside the slippery notion that you might have been thinking "fat thoughts" even though you didn't know you were thinking those thoughts, which is a great way for Byrne to cover her ass. How about the loopy idea that thinking "thin thoughts" makes it impossible for you to be overweight? Really? Even if you're suffering from a medical condition that causes you to be overweight, or your body type is predisposed to being a little heavier? You can overcome that by thinking "thin thoughts"?

That's right, says Byrne.

"Whether people have been told they have a slow thyroid, a slow metabolism or their body size is hereditary, these are all disguises for thinking 'fat thoughts.' If you accept any of those conditions as applicable to you . . . you will continue to [be] overweight."

So tell the doctor to screw off, get your mind right, and feel free to hit the drive-through window at McDonald's!

Byrne: "The most common thought that people hold, and I held it too, is that food was responsible for my weight gain. That is a belief that does not serve you, and in my mind now it is complete balderdash! Food is not responsible for putting on weight. It is your *thought* that food is responsible for putting on weight that actually has food put on weight. . . . Food cannot cause you to put on weight, unless you *think* it can."

After "beefing up" to "a hefty 143 pounds," the small-framed Byrne says she now maintains "my perfect weight of 116 pounds and I can eat whatever I want."

In that case, I have a challenge for Byrne: Let's see her eat whatever she wants for a month, as long as that menu includes three big meals a day, plus snacks, plus desserts. At the end of the month, if she hasn't gained a pound, I'll eat page 62 of my copy of *The Secret*.

Byrne even advises shunning overweight people:

"If you see people who are overweight, do not observe them, but immediately switch your mind to the picture of you in your perfect body and feel it."

That might be a bit hard if the overweight people in your life include your mom or your spouse or your best friend or your boss—but hey, you're trying to think "thin thoughts," so those relationships might have to suffer for the time being, what with you not even observing these folks.

According to *The Secret*, you can manipulate the universe to get things you want. The DVD version shows a woman ogling a necklace in a store window. She thinks and wishes real hard—and presto! She's wearing the necklace. (I believe that trick was first performed on the third season of *Bewitched*. Or was it *I Dream of Jeannie*?)

"A ten-year-old boy named Colin . . . had seen and loved 'The Secret,'" begins one story in the book. "Colin's family made a week-long visit to Disney World, and on their first day they experienced long lines at the park. So that night, just before Colin fell asleep, he thought, 'Tomorrow, I'd love to go on all the big rides and never have to wait in line.'"

Hey, wait a minute—he was doing it wrong! You're not supposed to have negative thoughts about "never" having to do anything. It's all about the positive. *The Secret* isn't even consistent *in its own examples.*

According to the book, the law of attraction worked anyway. The next day Colin's family was chosen as Epcot's First Family of the Day, which meant they'd be escorted around the park by a staff member and given VIP passes entitling them to instant access to all rides—no waiting in lines.

But what if six other kids at Disney that day had watched *The Secret* on DVD and had wished with equal fervor for all-access treatment? Why did Colin "win"? Not to mention the fact that a 10-year-old is being taught to harbor selfish wishes. Wouldn't it be nice if he wished that some other kid—maybe a sick kid going through some rough times—would get to "go on all the big rides and never have to wait in line"?

One of the big keys to The Secret seems to be getting yourself into an extremely selfish mindset, 24/7.

Even more insidious than the just-wish-for-it mentality is the explicitly stated belief that if bad things happen to you, it's your own damned fault. According to the teachers of The Secret, if you're broke it's because you have too many negative thoughts keeping money from reaching you, and if you're sick it's because you believed you could become sick. Without exception, everyone deserves what he or she gets.

This is a stunningly odious philosophy. Are we truly to believe that children born with life-shortening illnesses, that victims of terrorism and genocide, that starving families in Africa should blame themselves for their godforsaken bad fortune? Tell the widow of a 9/11 victim or the mother of a child with cancer or the father who has just buried his seven-year-old son who was struck and killed by a car that if only those victims had believed in the law of attraction, they would have been just fine. Go ahead, tell them.

"You cannot 'catch' anything unless you think you can, and thinking you can is inviting it to you with your thought," says *The Secret.*

And: "Disease cannot live in a body that's in a healthy emotional state."

And: "You don't have to fight to get rid of a disease. Just the simple process of letting go of negative thoughts will allow your natural state of health to emerge within you. And your body will heal itself."

Seabiscuit's stall never contained so much horseshit. You can be the all-time master of positive thought—and you still might get cancer or have a stroke or suffer a heart attack. Every positive thinker and great leader in the history of the world has eventually died from something. How could that happen if they were acting as magnets of positive energy?

Not only does *The Secret* tell you that you can achieve wealth, success, and even love through positive thoughts—it also says you shouldn't dwell on the negative, even if you're trying to change the negative, because that will just add more energy to that downer of a situation.

According to the book, protesting a war "creates more war." If you're angry about human suffering, you're contributing to that suffering by adding extra energy to it.

"The anti-drug movement has actually created more drugs," claims the book. "Because we're focusing on what we don't want—drugs!"

This is the book Oprah has blessed with two full shows. A book that tells you if you want something or someone, all you have to do is visualize it happening, and it will happen. A book that tells you not to observe fat people, lest their overweightness invade your thoughts. A book that says we should blame the victim—that if something shitty and tragic happens to you, you had it coming. A book that says you shouldn't get involved in fighting injustice, because it only adds to the injustice.

I believe there's nothing wrong with a little positive thinking. Hell, there's nothing wrong with a *lot* of positive thinking. If you dwell on the negative all the time, if you walk around with a spiritual black cloud over your head, of course you're going to make your own life and the lives of others more difficult.

But I don't know how anyone can keep a straight face while selling The Secret. The world is filled with positive people who never get out from under a lifetime of pain and disappointment—and miserable bastards who catch one lucky break after another.

There really *is* a conspiracy at work here. It's not a conspiracy of enlightened leaders who know the secret of the universe is the law of attraction; it's the conspiracy of self-help hucksters to sell all these cheap, warmed-over ideas to people who are so desperate to believe in quick-fix, New Age "solutions" that they'll believe all this bullshit.

14

BEWARE OF FALSE
IDOL VOTES

The votes were rigged last week. . . . They don't want the
Final Five to be all-female. Haley is almost as popular as
Sanjaya, and is the only cute rural white girl-next-door
type with nice legs. Haley and Sanjaya bring in the
viewers.

—*American Idol* fan "Ed," positing his conspiracy
theories in a comments section on the
Reality TV Web site in 2007

He was just 17 and he looked even younger. Russian women
have fuller mustaches.

His hair was unlike anything we'd ever seen.

He made the girls cry, and the ladies swoon.

He had a name you couldn't forget.

And when he sang—

Well, when he sang, hell had a name.

Dogs whimpered in put-me-out-of-my-misery agony, window-
panes shattered, and music lovers the world over winced as if they
had just bitten their own tongues while eating a bad potato chip.

They called him *Sanjaya*, and for a glorious multiweek stretch
in spring 2007, he threatened to bring down the juggernaut known

as *American Idol*. For if the talent-free Sanjaya could win the big prize, what was the point of watching this show?

It was one thing for the magnificently talented Jennifer Hudson to get booted from the show a bit prematurely, or for the barely adequate Nikki McKibbin to survive longer than the gifted Tamyra Gray—but if a tone-deaf national joke with less vocal ability than the winner of the Tuesday Night Karaoke Contest & Chicken Buffet at your local neighborhood tavern was crowned the next big thing in pop music, *American Idol* would lose even the pretense of credibility.

Yet week after week, Sanjaya survived.

Was it shock jock Howard Stern, urging his army of listeners to vote for Sanjaya with all their technical might? Was it the subversive "Vote for the Worst" Web site, which encouraged fans to screw with the process by casting votes for the least talented finalist?

Or was it something darker? Could it be the *American Idol* producers wanted Sanjaya around and were jimmying the result, as the aforementioned "Ed" asserted on the Reality TV Web site?

In the first half of the first decade of the 21st century, the biggest phenomenon in all of television wasn't *The Sopranos* or *Lost* or *24* or *Desperate Housewives*, nor was it an adventure reality show such as *Survivor* or *The Amazing Race*. It was a glorified talent contest called *American Idol*, which was really nothing more than an updated version of the hokey old *Star Search* show, with amateurs competing to become instant celebrities. (Decades before *Star Search*, there were programs such as *Ted Mack's Amateur Hour* on TV, and even before that, amateur talent contests on radio. They probably had an *Amateur Hour* during the Middle Ages.)

Literally tens of millions of viewers tuned in every week to see a group of moderately talented amateur singers belt out cover versions of middle-of-the-road hits, usually from the 1960s and 1970s. They didn't even have a live band on the tacky stage most of the time, for crying out loud. Everybody sang along to recorded music tracks.

From this cheesiness sprang a phenomenon. Ryan Seacrest was crowned the next Dick Clark. (In the meantime, Seacrest's cohost from season 1 of *American Idol*, one Brian Dunkleman, seemed to spend the next several years in the same showbiz limbo that had claimed the likes of McLean Stevenson and Shelley Long in years gone by.) Simon Cowell became one of the most famous and highly paid personalities in the world. Randy Jackson's witless and repetitive "Yo Dawg" became a national catch phrase. The entertainment shows and magazines breathlessly chronicled Paula Abdul's fragile wackiness. Paula even got a reality show of her own.

Most astonishing of all, many *AI* winners—and even some also-rans—became genuine music stars, on a par with the biggest names in pop music. Kelly Clarkson, Clay Aiken, Carrie Underwood, and Chris Daughtry segued from talent show contestants to legitimate, award-winning, platinum-selling artists. Jennifer Hudson won an Academy Award for best supporting actress in the musical *Dreamgirls*. Fantasia Barrino starred in *The Color Purple* on Broadway.

Other winners and finalists were quickly forgotten and turned bitter. There were more than a few scandals involving criminal or lascivious behavior on the part of some finalists, not to mention the allegations by one contestant that he'd slept with Paula. But none of these setbacks made a dent in the *AI* juggernaut.

The only real and ongoing threat to the show's success: the dogged rumors that the voting was rigged.

You don't have to be a conspiracy theorist to believe the voting process on American Idol is flawed. That's because it *is* flawed.

First and most problematic, you can vote as often as the technology allows. In fact, they *want* you to vote as often as you can, because every call and every text message is another "ka-ching!" for the cash register. If they limited it to one vote per viewer, it would be more expensive to ensure the rules were followed—and less profitable. That's not going to happen.

But when you open the phone lines to an entire nation for a two-hour period (staggered across time zones), you're also opening your voting process to myriad technical headaches.

First, not all the votes get counted. Even if 30 million votes get through, untold millions of other potential votes are thwarted by busy signals. Luck is a huge factor.

So is techno-expertise. Whereas a potential phone call will die with a busy signal—you have to dial again to get through—text messages line up one behind the other, like motorists at the DMV. It may take a while for you to reach the finish line, but you will get there. In addition, the very process of text messaging takes up much less "space" on a phone line, so it's easier to get through. What this means is text messaging has the advantage over old-fashioned dialing.

Unless, that is, you're using computerized auto-dialing devices, capable of casting hundreds of votes in the time it would take a human dialer to get through just once. Just a few hundred of these so-called phone phreakers can tilt the vote—especially if it's a particularly close finale, as in season 2, when Ruben Studdard clipped Clay Aiken by less than 1 percent of the vote.

American Idol producers say they have safeguards in place to detect phone phreaking, but there's software out there that supposedly enables the phone phreakers to dodge those barricades. So it goes in the world of hacking and attacking. Just when you come up with a tamperproof system, some rascal-genius figures out a way around it. If all the hackers in the world put their brainpower to more important causes, they probably could have solved global warming by now.

"Can 'American Idol' Voting Be Fixed?" was the headline on a story on the Associated Content Web site in 2007. Kari Livingston wrote:

It happens every season. One contestant is voted off or banished to the bottom two while the country gasps in shock. In season one Tamyra Gray was ousted while Nikki McKibbin was sent back to safety. In the second season, Joshua Gracin was safe after a terrible performance while mini-diva Trenyce received a one-way ticket home to Memphis. Jennifer Hudson was the sixth to go in season three, while red-headed crooner John Stevens lived to warble another week. In season four, inexplicable heartthrob Constantine Maroulis was booted off before Scott Savol, and in the shocker of all shockers, fan favorite Chris Daughtry finished in fourth place when many fans expected him to win it all.

The article details past snafus, including a power outage in Chicago that prevented Jennifer Hudson's hometown fans from voting for her, and the claim from thousands of Daughtry fans that when they voted for their man, they heard Katherine McPhee's voice thanking them for their vote.

An online petition calls for changes in the system.

Instead of being a talent contest...it has turned into "which fan base can cheat through their votes faster." It has surfaced that there are different Internet programs that will allow you to get in thousands of votes, change your time zone so you can vote for triple the amount of time...there are also ways to get thousands of votes through [via] text messaging. Your disclaimer claims that power voting is not allowed and those votes will be thrown out, however it is very difficult to determine these methods by which the power voting occurs....

There should be a limit of five votes per phone number and 10 text messages per phone number.... There will always be those who feel the need to cheat or exploit the system but this could cut down on that dramatically....

In fact, some televised talent shows *do* limit the number of calls and texts—but don't hold your breath waiting for *American Idol* to follow suit. If it did so at this juncture, some conspiracy theorists would point to the change as proof that the votes were manipulated in the past.

AI fan sites are filled with complaints from viewers who say that no matter how often they try, they can never get through. Is this bad luck, or are darker forces at work?

A DVD titled *American Idol Unauthorized* makes the very wobbly claim that the producers of the show decide who's going to win—and then jam the phone lines to ensure their choices come out on top. There are lots of interviews with disgruntled former contestants, such as the weasely Corey Clark, who allegedly had an affair with Paula Abdul.

"The voting system is rigged up!" says Corey, who then offers no proof of his claim.

We also hear from "experts" including former contestants on *Fear Factor* and *Survivor*, a Beverly Hills "media psychiatrist," and the guy who plays Ari's flamboyant assistant Lloyd on *Entourage*. I'm not kidding. They don't make claims that the show is being rigged; they're just on the DVD because—well, there's no good reason for them to be there.

American Idol Unauthorized is filled with damning statements—one magazine editor flat out says that the show is rigged and everyone knows it—but there's not one piece of hard evidence on the DVD.

It would be hard to dispute the argument that the efforts of Howard Stern and the "Vote for the Worst" campaign resulted in thousands if not millions of votes for the talent-impaired Sanjaya. But let's not discount the kid's popularity with the little girls, the suburban moms, and the show tune–loving folks who make up a huge portion of the *AI* fan base. Lousy voice notwithstanding, Sanjaya was extremely viewer friendly. (His hair had more personality than he did, but still . . .)

It would also be impossible to dispute that the *American Idol* voting system is more flawed than Florida's circa 2000 and that the most popular contestant won't necessarily gather the most votes. The process is a giant and glorious mess, and it's probably impossible to fix it at this point.

But does any of this mean the producers of the show are actually rigging the results? Hardly. Even with all the reports of voting snafus and technical glitches, of power voting and "Vote for the Worst" campaigns, there's never been any evidence linking anyone at Fox with vote tampering.

Why would they? In season 6, *American Idol* was bringing in some 32 million viewers a week—more than 10 million viewers above the respective totals for such hits as *CSI*, *Desperate Housewives*, and *Dancing with the Stars*. The show is in a league of its own. Why would the producers risk millions upon millions of dollars on some kind of vote-rigging scheme when it really doesn't matter who wins? (Unless it was Sanjaya.)

As long as the finalists include a mix of the gorgeous and the weight-challenged, various ethnic groups, hunky guys and cute girls, with the occasional oddball favorite, the viewers will be there. As long as we get the offstage dramas and the onstage tears, the standing ovations from the crowd and the snarky comments from Simon, the viewers will be there.

Even if the producers wanted to finesse the results, thereby risking international embarrassment, there's no guarantee their choices would be any more appealing than the results we're getting with an admittedly screwed-up system.

The voting process on *American Idol* is unarguably problematic. But just because something is flawed doesn't mean somebody "fixed" it.

V

BUSINESS

15

I'LL HAVE AN ICED GRANDE VANILLA NONFAT CONSPIRACY

I think if a Starbucks is coming into your town, and it's the first Starbucks and some people who don't like it decide, "We're going to do something to prevent this Starbucks from being built"—then I think that could be tactically sound. I'm not saying that people should do it, but it does make some tactical sense.

—From an interview with Josh Wolf, self-described anarchist sympathizer, on the 10 Zen Monkeys Web site

More than any other chain or franchise this side of Wal-Mart, the Starbucks name elicits visceral reactions among self-appointed crusaders for human rights and creative expression.

The anti-Starbucks crowd believes that the ubiquitous mermaid logo is the sign of the beast and that every time a Starbucks goes up, a neighborhood loses a little bit of its soul. Even if a Starbucks replaced a two-flat occupied by a crack whore on the second floor and a drug-dealing serial killer on the first floor, the Starbucks haters slap their foreheads and bellow, "There goes the neighborhood!"

We've seen the footage of protesters at World Trade Organization conferences, throwing rocks through the windows of Starbucks (and maybe the Gap if there's a handy Gap within rock-throwing distance).

I'll acknowledge there are times the Starbucks experience can be trying. I once ordered an iced Venti nonfat latte in a Manhattan Starbucks, heard my drink called out—and there on the counter was a large cup filled with milk and ice, no espresso. When I pointed out to the barista guy that he had forgotten to include the espresso part of the equation, he looked me in the eye and insisted that he had made the drink correctly and that all I had to do was shake it. When I did so and the drink remained milky white, he reluctantly took it from me and said he'd make me another one, but warned that it would look the same. It didn't—mainly because this time he actually put espresso in the drink. I walked out of there fully expecting Ashton Kutcher to tell me I'd been punk'd.

And there are times when Starbucks does seem to be controlling the universe. I remember when I used to visit New York City in the 1990s, and I'd call around to find out where the nearest Starbucks might be. Now when I'm in Manhattan, I don't even bother asking the hotel doorman for directions to the nearest Starbucks. I just start walking, knowing I'll bump into one within a block, two blocks at the most.

Using the "Store Locator" device on the Starbucks Web site, I find that in Chicago there are 73 Starbucks outlets within a two-mile radius of my downtown address. The comedian Lewis Black has a routine about a "Starbucks across the street from a Starbucks," saying, "Ladies and gentlemen, that is the end of the universe"—but it's no exaggeration. In fact there's a Web site detailing all the intersections in the world where one Starbucks sits across from another.

They sell coffee, breakfast snacks, sandwiches, salads. Trendy, eco-friendly bottled water called Ethos. Christmas ornaments. Music. Coffeemakers. Cups and mugs and thermoses and plates and all sorts of other stuff. At times it's hard to figure out what's for sale and what's part of the decor.

How did Paul McCartney score his bestselling CD in 10 years? With a great helping hand from Starbucks. Every time you walked into a Starbucks in summer 2007, you saw copies of McCartney's *Memory Almost Full*. It was the first release from the Hear Music label formed by Starbucks and the Concord Music Group.

The inspirational movie *Akeelah and the Bee*? A Starbucks production. You could find the DVD at Starbucks registers, next to *A Long Way Gone*, the bestselling book about a boy soldier in Sierra Leone.

When a company is that successful, that powerful, that ubiquitous, that self-righteous, and it just keeps growing and growing and growing—there's bound to be a backlash.

But this is not a book about international labor practices or how various companies treat their employees, or whether Starbucks actually puts small coffee shops out of business. For every person who swears Starbucks is the Evil Empire—a cold-hearted machine that mistreats its employees and serves up overpriced, mediocre beverages—you can find someone who tells you Starbucks is a great place to work, has a relatively strong track record with coffee bean farmers, and is incredibly popular because it makes great coffee. (Personally, I'm never in a Starbucks more than twice a day. Three times max.) We're here to talk about conspiracies and urban legends—and because Starbucks is so ubiquitous and so controversial, it has been the target of a number of negative, Internet-fueled stories. Some are true, some are sorta-kinda accurate, and many are 100 percent, unadulterated nonsense.

Let's separate the shots of truth from the Venti servings of lies.

1. Starbucks is closing all its stores in Israel for political reasons.

According to a widely circulated e-mail, Starbucks was joining an Arab boycott of American businesses by shutting down its operations in Israel.

In fact, Starbucks *did* close its six stores in Israel—for economic, not political, reasons. With help from the Anti-Defamation

League, Starbucks went on the counterattack to put an end to the e-mail rumor.

Verdict: True, but not for the reasons claimed by the conspiracy theories.

2. A Starbucks in New York City charged 9/11 rescue workers for cases of water.

Numerous media organizations reported the story of the employees of an ambulance service going into a Starbucks store on 9/11, asking for cases of water—and being presented with a bill for $130. The workers paid for the water with money from their own pockets.

The story made huge waves on the Internet, presumably circulated by the anti-Starbucks crowd as further evidence of the company's callous, profit-first mode of operation.

In this case, the reports were accurate. A refund check of $130 was eventually issued to the ambulance company.

It should be noted that other Starbucks in the area provided free coffee and water to rescue workers on 9/11, and the company donated $1 million to 9/11 funds. But the lingering memory for many was that one numbskull employee charging rescue workers for bottled water on the worst day in the history of New York City.

Verdict: True.

3. Starbucks pays shameful wages to Central American farmers.

According to an article in the *Willamette Week Online*, specialty coffee accounts for only 7 percent of the global coffee market, while "40 percent of all coffee is bought by four companies—Nestle, Procter & Gamble, Kraft, and Sara Lee—who pay a paltry 50 cents per pound for their beans. This often doesn't even cover the farmers' costs of production. In comparison, Starbucks paid an average of $1.20 per pound [in 2006]."

Verdict: False.

4. Starbucks is against the war in Iraq and won't do anything to support the troops.

U.S. Marine Corps sergeant Howard C. Wright authored one of the most widely circulated e-mails of the 21st century, in which he urged Americans to boycott Starbucks:

Recently Marines over in Iraq supporting this country...wrote to Starbucks because they wanted to let them know how much they liked their coffee and wanted to score some free coffee grounds. Starbucks wrote back telling the Marines thanks for their support...but they don't support the war and anyone in it and they won't send them the coffee.

So as not to offend them we should not support buying any Starbucks products. As a war veteran...writing to you patriots I feel we should get this out in the open.
Semper Fidelis
Sgt. Howard C. Wright
1st Force Recon Co.
1st Plt. PLT RTO

As Starbucks explained to Sgt. Wright, company policy authorizes donations only to official public charities, libraries, and schools. They also pointed out that they encourage employees to donate their free pound of coffee each week to troops overseas—but that choice is up to each individual employee.

Sgt. Wright composed a second e-mail, which received nowhere near the attention of the first one.

Dear Readers,
I did a wrong thing that needs to be cleared up. I heard by word of mouth about how Starbucks said they didn't support the war ...[and I] didn't do my research properly like I should have.

This is not true. Starbucks supports the men and women in uniform. They have personally contacted me.

Now I ask that you all pass this email around to everyone....

Applause to Sgt. Wright for taking steps to set things right. But as we all know, the correction rarely has the impact of the initial mistake, so it's reasonable to assume that far fewer people have seen letter #2 than have seen letter #1.

Verdict: False.

5. Starbucks is a tyrannical, uncaring employer.

As opposed to all those other service industry employers that lavish their full- and part-time workers with nothing but big checks, full health care, lots of scheduling flexibility, and endless love, right?

I think a lot of customers just assume it's hell working at Starbucks because the employees are often robotically cheerful as they're slaving away, yelling drink orders at one another and creating one complicated caffeinated beverage after another. Many Starbucks employees seem to be overqualified graduate students, or twentysomethings with advanced degrees who are stuck taking frappuccino orders from jerky business execs because they haven't found anything in their chosen field.

So they must hate their jobs, right?

I'm not so sure. *Fortune* magazine ranked Starbucks number 11 in the entire country in their 2005 list of the 100 best companies to work for. Some of the employees at my regular Starbucks haunts have been there for years. They tell me they like the gig because it gives them a steady income as they toil away on their screenplays or study for their master's degree or audition for acting jobs. Their cheerful attitude seems genuine, not forced. You'd almost think they took pride in their jobs and enjoyed what they're doing!

Shocking as that may seem.

If you work 20 hours or more per week at Starbucks, you get a health plan and a 401(k). How many other companies come through with similar benefits for part-time employees? There's also a partial tuition reimbursement plan.

I'm not drinking the Flavor Aid (or should I say the espresso?) when it comes to the Starbucks employee experience. I've never worked at a Starbucks. I'm sure there are thousands of Starbucks employees and ex-employees (Starbucks calls them "partners" rather than employees) who could tell you why working there sucks—and thousands who would argue otherwise.

But if Starbucks is such a hellhole to work at, why is it that none of its stores ever seem to have to close down for lack of employees? *Verdict: False.*

6. In the future, Starbucks will offer sexual favors.

Uh, that's a joke in the cult movie *Idiocracy*. Luke Wilson travels to the future and sees a Starbucks advertising insanely expensive coffee drinks ("Latte, $200"), as well as some specialty drinks—for example, "Full Body Latte, $50,000."

Verdict: To be determined.

16

RUMMY AND THE BIRD FLU

Somewhere, I imagine, there's a small group of people proud to be counted among the Friends of Avian Flu, or FAF for short. I suspect they have a catchy statement, such as "Keeping the nightmare alive" . . . their challenge is to keep the bird flu forever in the public eye.

—British Medical Journal *article downplaying bird flu worries, June 30, 2007*

It was like something out of a conspiracy movie.

A deadly, bird-transmitted virus was about to sweep the world—and the secretary of defense of the United States just happened to have substantial holdings in the company making the very product that just might put a dent in the pandemic.

How convenient.

In an e-mail labeled "BIRD FLU—U.S. PROPAGANDA!" the conspiracy theorists laid out the "facts," so to speak. A truncated version of the e-mail that surfaced in 2006:

Do you know that "bird flu" was discovered in Vietnam 9 years ago?

Do you know that barely 100 people have died in the whole world in all that time?

135

Do you know it was the Americans who alerted us to the efficiency of the human anti-viral Tamiflu as a preventative?

Do you know that Tamiflu barely alleviates some symptoms of the common flu?

Do you know who markets Tamiflu?

Roche Laboratories.

Do you know who bought the patent for Tamiflu from Roche Laboratories in 1996?

Gilead Sciences Inc.

Do you know who was then president of Gilead Sciences Inc. and remains a major shareholder?

Donald Rumsfeld, the Secretary of Defence of the USA.

Do you know that sales of Tamiflu were over $254 million in 2004 and more than $1 billion in 2005?

Do you know how many more millions Roche can earn in the coming months if the business of fear continues?

President's Bush's friends decide that Tamiflu is the solution for a pandemic that has not yet occurred and has caused a hundred deaths worldwide in 9 years. This medicine doesn't so much as cure the common flu. So we end up paying for medicine while Rumsfeld, Cheney and Bush get richer. Thank the RED states!

I'll say this: Unlike some conspiracy theories (e.g., the faked moon landing), this one isn't a wild fantasy concocted and perpetuated by paranoid minds. That said, there are some errors and some holes in the bird flu panic conspiracy.

We were never really sure—we're *still* not sure—how scared we should be about this whole bird flu thing. It's a very real virus, and there is still concern that it could become a pandemic, especially in some third world countries.

In June 2007, scientists and researchers met for a three-day conference in Rome to assess the bird flu problem.

"In most cases the virus is rapidly detected and kept under control, as most countries are equipped with improved response systems," said a story from the Associated Press.

"However, in nations that combine a high density of population and unsafe poultry management, the situation remains serious."

As of this writing, the H5N1 strain of bird flu has killed nearly 200 people and has seriously depleted poultry stocks worldwide.

"Experts fear that the virus could mutate into a form easily spread between people, potentially igniting a flu pandemic," said the AP.

That's what we've been hearing for a few years now—that there's the potential for a pandemic. And that's what has doctors, scientists, and the media treading the tricky border between responsible reporting on a possible danger, and panic peddling. So far, we haven't seen evidence of human-to-human transmission; everyone who contracted the virus had extensive contact with infected birds.

But there is the possibility of a mutated, stronger strain of the virus.

Let's take a look at the claims that Rumsfeld and his pals orchestrated some kind of conspiracy to push bird flu panic—and cash in on the public's worries.

First, the bird flu was discovered in humans in Hong Kong, not Vietnam. However, the death toll listed in the e-mail was pretty accurate for the time, and it is true that "the Americans"—that is, the Centers for Disease Control—named Tamiflu as a possible treatment for avian flu.

As for the charge that Tamiflu "barely alleviates" common flu symptoms—the drug is designed to go after the virus itself, not to alleviate symptoms. Nevertheless, it actually has proven to be effective in alleviating some flu symptoms some of the time. As of this writing, Tamiflu's effectiveness in combating bird flu in humans has not been 100 percent determined.

It is true that Rumsfeld holds a substantial number of shares in the company that produces Tamiflu, that he has profited from this association and would profit even more if there were a bird flu pandemic. It would be in his best financial interest if every family in the world stocked up on Tamiflu, just in case.

Rumsfeld urged President Ford to develop a swine flu vaccine in the 1970s—and the vaccination program caused thousands of cases of paralysis and dozens of deaths (more people actually died from the vaccine than from the swine flu itself). In the 1980s he was president of the company that owned the patent on aspartame, and he used his clout to get long-denied FDA approval for the controversial artificial sweetener.

And he sold us a load of horseshit about the Iraq War in the 2000s.

So it's difficult to dismiss the bird flu conspiracy out of hand—but there exists no proof that Rumsfeld deliberately exaggerated the bird flu situation just so he could make even more money. (He's already filthy rich.) He can't be that conscience-free, greedy, and ruthless, can he?

Rumsfeld recused himself from any administration decisions regarding Tamiflu. News reports said he didn't sell his shares because he didn't want to appear to be cashing in on the bird flu semipanic—but by hanging on to the shares, it could give the appearance that he felt the price of his stock would only go up.

Maybe Rummy's best move would have been to sell the shares—and to donate all the profits to medical research in third world countries. Sure, he might have been accused of cynical grandstanding, but so what? It could have been one of the few times in his long and controversial career when some folks would have said, "Nicely done, Rummy. Well played."

17

EVIAN IS NAIVE SPELLED BACKWARD

Four gallons of spring water (two gals. cold, two gals. room temperature), 8 oz. size is best for us. PLEASE NO EVIAN WATER.

—From the contract rider for Styx (the current version, not the real, Dennis DeYoung version), as reported by the Smoking Gun

Pick up a copy of *Us Weekly* or *People* or *InTouch* or *Star*, or log on to any celebrity-obsessed Web site, and you're bound to find a picture of some fetching starlet scooting someplace while wearing overpriced, oversized sunglasses while clutching two must-have survival devices:

1. A cell phone and/or personal communications device.
2. Bottled water.

It's amazing. Stars of the 21st century are really, really, really thirsty.

Whether they're at LAX or exiting a health club, taking their toddlers for a walk or meeting Orlando Bloom for a salad at the Ivy, they must have bottled water! Pioneering women of the 19th century made it across the Great Plains with the occasional slug from a canteen or slurp from a friendly river, but Jessica Simpson can't make it down her driveway without a giant bottle of Fiji.

Jennifer Aniston signed a huge contract with a bottled water giant and was seen toting the bottles everywhere, label conveniently facing out. What, she didn't make enough money on *Friends*?

When the bottled water craze first reached us, Evian seemed to be the brand of choice. But just as beers such as Budweiser and Miller have been "out-cooled" by the likes of Heineken Light and Stella Artois, Evian now seems very Madonna in her *Truth or Dare* phase compared with trendy bottled waters such as Volvic and Smartwater and Voss.

In fact, some celebrities specifically request any water *but* Evian, according to reports.

From the "Ask the Answer Bitch" column* on E! online:

Why do most celebrities demand no Evian when requesting bottled water? —Kara, Pittsburgh.

The Bitch Replies: The most likely reason has to do with rumors involving nuclear disaster.... According to top celebrity caterer David Mintz in Toronto, stars are simply turning towards other brands, specifically Fiji or the Norwegian water known as Voss....

Both Ashlee Simpson and her ex, the delightfully spiky Ryan Cabrera, cannot stand Evian in their dressing rooms, according to news reports. Ditto with Clay Aiken and the Red Hot Chili Peppers, whose contract rider reportedly states, "no Evian or other local spring water." (The band instead prefers water culled from a still glacier.)

---

*I have a few questions of my own for the Answer Bitch.

1. Did you study journalism, and if so, would you say working as the Answer Bitch means your education was worth it?
2. Do you remember the excitement you felt when you called your parents to tell them you'd gotten the job as the Answer Bitch?
3. When filling out your income tax form, under "Occupation," do you write, "Answer Bitch"?

Just wondering.

But the most fascinating anti-Evian theory comes from top on-set caterer Tom Morales, [whose company] provides food to about 25 movie sets a year. Morales also has worked thousands of music concerts. . . .

According to Morales, the no-Evian clause is a holdover from years ago, when a rumor started circulating that the radiation cloud from the 1986 Chernobyl nuclear disaster blew straight from the Ukraine to Evian's water source in France.

Not true, of course. Nor is it true that the makers of Evian so named their product as a dig at stupid consumers willing to pay big money for water, which is readily available via your kitchen sink. ("*Evian* is *Naive* spelled backward!") As a rule, companies try not to risk their entire existence on in-jokes.

Of course, it could be argued that anyone who buys bottled water is indeed naive, and I'm counting myself in that group. We live in a world in which most people would be thrilled to be drinking American tap water—yet those of us who have access to the best from-the-faucet water are the very ones who spend as much as $2 for a bottle of water from some faraway glacier or magical spring.

"[Bottled water] is more expensive than gasoline," consumer advocate John Stossel noted in an interview on *The O'Reilly Factor*.

"We ran taste tests, and tap water in almost all parts of the country beats the bottled water, especially the bestseller, Evian, which is *Naive* spelled backwards, for good reason."

On a classic episode of *Penn & Teller: Bullshit!* the illusionists filled bottles with water from a garden hose behind a restaurant and then passed off the bottles as expensive designer water. Customers at the high-end restaurant actually noted the difference between various "brands," even though it was all the same water, from the same tap. I'd make fun of this, except I probably would have noticed those same differences in taste in the same situation.

Americans spend some *10 billion dollars a year* on bottled water, according to the Beverage Marketing Corporation.

Perhaps we need a stronger word than "naive" to categorize such madness. Is there a brand of bottled water called Stoidi?

VI

MIRACLES

18

DEAD MAN TALKING!

By entering the stage area, you're agreeing to be "read" by John. John cannot control who "comes through." So there are no "passive audience members." For instance, John has read the cameraman, soundman and someone in the next room during rehearsals. If you feel you'll be too embarrassed, too frazzled, or just not interested, we ask that you give up your seat to someone who's anxious for a reading.

—From the guidelines for guests entering studio tapings for John Edward's *Crossing Over* television show

There is absolutely no doubt in my mind that some of us have the ability to speak to the dead.

Heck, I believe *all* of us have the ability to communicate with the dead. You can do it right now! Say hello to John the Baptist, let Shakespeare know you've always admired his work, tell Hitler to f—— off. Give your best to some dead loved ones while you're at it.

That part—talking to the dead—is easy. It's the getting-a-response part that's a little tricky.

For many, the desire to communicate with the dead and to discover some "proof" of a life beyond this world is so strong that we want to believe certain mortals among us possess "psychic abilities." These so-called mediums act as conduits between this life and the afterlife, receiving signals and clues and messages from those who have passed on before us and are now apparently engaged in some kind of ethereal game of charades.

"I'm getting a 'C,'" the slick-talking psychic will say as he walks around the room, scanning the audience for someone who was close to someone whose name included a 'C.' (Gee, what are the odds?)

"The name could be Charles, or Carol, something with a C, could be a last name like Charles or something with a 'Ch,' a grandmother or a mother, she died in the hospital after a long illness . . ."

And then some poor woman in the audience will raise her hand and say, "That might be my grandmother! Her maiden name was Charlton and she died in the hospital after being sick for months!"

Lord save us, it's a miracle.

Here's what gets me. If your grandmother wants to let you know she forgives you for that big fight you had just before she croaked, why does she have to go through some jabbering TV host with gelled hair and a perma-tan? Why can't she just tell you directly?

Oh, that's right. Because the TV huckster has the gift, and you don't.

Let me say right here that I'm a believer who doesn't believe.

I do believe and hope there's something out there beyond our time on Earth—but I don't believe that women with tarot cards who work out of their kitchens and men with $120 haircuts who have shows on basic cable channels have some sort of special ability to receive signals from the dead.

I believe their gift is the ability to do either "cold readings" (time-tested questioning techniques) and/or "hot readings" (gathering information prior to a session) in order to glean enough information from their victims, I mean clients, to make it seem as if they're actually communicating with a deceased loved one.

On some level I hope I'm wrong about this. Because if psychics and mediums have no special gift, and they know they have no special gift, and they're using tactics to con people into thinking they're engaging in a dialogue with a dead loved one—often reducing these clients to pools of tears—that's redefining cynical exploitation. That's white-hot despicable.

In 2007, I took a look at the work of Sylvia Browne, one of the most successful psychics of her generation. Her numerous bestsellers include *A Psychic's Tour of the Afterlife* and *Christmas in Heaven*. In the latter book, Browne addresses such questions as "Do heavenly spirits decorate?" and "Are there presents and exchanging of gifts?" If the answer to either of these questions is "Yes," I guess that means they must have Wal-Marts and Costcos in the afterlife. And credit cards. And electrical outlets so you can plug in those decorations.

Browne has been a frequent guest with Larry King and Montel Williams. There's an infamous clip on the Internet showing one of her less successful readings on Montel's shows, in which Browne tells a woman, "The reason you couldn't find [your husband] is he's in the water." Browne continues to insist there was water involved in the man's death—even after the woman says that, no, he was a firefighter killed on 9/11.

"It doesn't matter anyway, honey," Browne says in a dismissive, cruel tone, obviously hoping to move on quickly from this public humiliation, "because he's still over there."

In another infamous gaffe, Browne told the family of a missing boy named Shawn Hornbeck that the boy was dead—and offered to help find his body for her usual fee of some $700 an hour.

The boy was found alive. Without Browne's help.

Then there was the time Browne appeared on a live radio show as a report came in that a group of trapped coal miners in West Virginia was alive. Immediately, Browne said she "knew" they were fine.

Sadly, that initial report turned out to be untrue. All but one of the miners was dead.

Unfortunately for Browne, she was still on the live program when that tragic news was delivered.

"I don't think there's anybody alive, maybe one," she said.

This is another gift you'll find in most psychics: the ability to roll with the punches and shift the story at the snap of your fingers without ever feeling bad about telling parents their missing kid is dead, or being wrong about the number of people dead in a developing news story.

Eerie, isn't it?

What about those TV stars such as John Edward who seem to have an uncanny ability to tell you things about your dead friend or grandma or spouse that they couldn't possibly have known beforehand?

As we have learned from shows such as Penn and Teller's work of genius *Bullshit!*, professional skeptics such as James Randi, and Web sites such as SkepticReport (www.skepticreport.com), TV psychics employ myriad techniques to extract information from subjects before and during taping sessions and live tour appearances.

One of the favored techniques is to gather the audience well in advance of the psychic's appearance. You have to be at the studio an hour or two before the actual taping begins, you have to be in line at the bookstore, you have to file into the auditorium long before the scheduled start time.

And what do you do during all that down time? You talk. And what do you talk about? The deceased loved one you're hoping to contact.

Perhaps there are microphones in strategic places. (In a TV studio, the microphones wouldn't even have to be hidden. The same mikes used to pick up your applause could be turned on well in advance of taping, to pick up snippets of conversation.) An easier approach would be for the psychic to have a few associates sprinkled through the crowd, posing as regular folks while extracting and gathering information.

There's also a strong possibility you'll be asked to fill out a questionnaire—a release form giving permission for your name and image to be used on the show or on the psychic's Web site. The information you provide might seem quite basic—but in the hands of an experienced reader, every little tidbit helps.

Once the psychic appears and starts his shtick, the game is on. His repertoire will include fast patter, a strong knowledge of demographics and statistical probabilities, the technique of framing questions as statements, and the ability to nimbly step past incorrect guesses quickly. He'll say things like "This might sound crazy, but is there anyone with a connection to a flood, some kind of flooding?" or "I know this sounds weird, but I'm getting something about someone who was a pilot or loved flying, maybe they were in the Air Force," or "Somebody here lost someone who lived in Paris for a while?"

You put 150 people in a room, you're going to get a hit.

Or he'll throw a date out there.

"I'm seeing the middle of October—it might be October 17 or a date near then—it has great significance for you."

Let's say the psychic is addressing a 60-year-old woman with three children, four grandchildren, a husband, numerous aunts, uncles, nephews, nieces, friends, and so on, not to mention more than a few deceased loved ones. For crying out loud, it's almost a statistical certainty that someone in her life had a birthday or died or got married or had something significant happen on or around October 17.

Isn't it interesting that virtually all psychics get their information in the same manner? It's never straightforward; it's always in bits and pieces, with the psychic saying something like, "Okay, they're telling me something about a fishing boat, a boat of some kind; there was an incident once on a boat. Did you fish with your grandfather when you were a little boy? . . . OK, you took a cruise . . . and that was one of the happier times, and he wants you to know that when he thinks of you, he doesn't think about the disagreement that happened later in your life; he doesn't think about when he was in the hospital and he was sick—he thinks about that cruise you took . . ."

They always get their information in drips and drops—making for dramatic television, as the psychic gets warmer and warmer and the "sitter" gets more and more emotional, often tearing up before collapsing in a heap of grateful closure. The psychic often asks for help in "interpreting" his information—a neat trick that turns a semiaccurate factoid into an amazingly detailed scoop.

Another classic technique used by psychics—the old double negative. He'll say, "Your father didn't serve in the military, did he?"

If you say, "Yes," he proceeds quickly, saying, "That's what I was getting."

If you say, "No," he proceeds just as quickly, saying, "No, no, I didn't think so."

No matter what your answer, he's going to act as if he had it right—and he's just picked up another piece of useful information along the way.

Of course, the actual conversations can also be edited for TV, so we don't see all the mistakes and missteps made by the psychic. It looks as if he's as direct and precise as a prosecutor on an episode of *Law & Order*.

One also has to factor in the "willing audience" factor. The vast majority of people who take the time and effort to attend a taping of *Crossing Over with John Edward* or a reading by Sylvia Browne aren't there to "bust" the star—they're hoping to make contact with someone on the other side. If they're lucky enough to be tabbed by the medium, they're going to try to help out by supplying as much information as possible during the conversation.

The psychic will also use flattery to coax the subject. He never says, "Ooh, you're a cheap bastard and you were always very mean to your siblings when you were growing up." He says, "You are a very loving, generous person, and you were always the one who looked out for your siblings when you were growing up, am I right?" Flattery will get him everywhere. It's just another way to get the subject to say, "Hey, this guy is *good*."

When psychics are asked why they can't use their powers to explain *where* the dead are when they're making contact or why they can't use their abilities to predict winning lottery numbers or prevent tragedies, they always say the same thing:

"It doesn't work that way."

Why not? Why does it always work the same way? Who decided how it would "work"?

For that matter, why is it that when someone is given "the gift," he or she turns it into a profit-making enterprise consisting of TV shows and audiobooks and public speaking tours? Aren't these people *freaked out* by all those conversations with the dead, and aren't they a little wary of making millions from those talks?

Many of these psychics say they realized they had special abilities at a young age. You'd think at least some of them would be so blown away by this "gift" that they'd become monks or priests or spiritual gurus, instead of infomercial hucksters.

Unless, of course, the real gift is the ability and the willingness to bullshit the willing and the faithful.

PET PSYCHICS

Imagine filling out a tax form or a questionnaire and coming to the "Occupation" box—and writing down "Pet Psychic."

Now that takes guts.

The amazing thing isn't that someone can make a living by claiming the ability to communicate with pets—it's that dozens of people are making a living this way. Google "pet psychic" and you'll get listings for the famous TV pet psychic Sonya Fitzpatrick, among many others, including:

- Lisa Greene: "Communicates telepathically with all species of animals . . ."
- Barbara Morrison: "Having the natural ability as an Animal Psychic, I am able to communicate with the Animal Kingdom . . ."
- Charlene Boyd: "Renowned animal psychic lets your pets speak to you . . ."
- Kathy Paradise: "Communicate with animals living or deceased . . ."

Amazing. When I was kid, I'm not sure there was a single pet psychic in the world. Now, according to the Internet listings, there are dozens of women—it's a female-dominated field—who have the ability to communicate with animals, even the dead ones!

Many of these pet psychics don't even have to meet with you in person to take your money. They're happy to do a reading *over the phone*. I guess you just hand the receiver to Tippy or Mr. Fluffers and let the pet psychic take it from there.

This places us squarely in a world where *Dr. Doolittle* and *Ace Ventura: Pet Detective* are documentaries.

Do some animals possess remarkable personalities? Sure. Are some animals capable of heroic deeds? Absolutely. Is it possible for a human and a pet to have a special, unique bond? I don't doubt it for a second.

But the idea that a dead cat can speak to its former owner through a pet psychic or that a crabby hamster can explain to a pet psychic exactly why it's in a bad mood—that's less believable than a rerun of *Mr. Ed*. You can ascribe all sorts of human characteristics to your pet, but that's not reality—that's a Disney cartoon.

Wait a minute, I'm getting a signal from your dog . . . it's getting stronger . . . got it! He wants to let you know that he'd like more table scraps, that you don't have to do that little voice when you talk to him, and that you don't have to ask him, "Want to go outside?" or "Do you want a treat?"—because the answer is always going to be "Yes!"

Sometimes my psychic powers frighten even me.

19

IT'S A MIRACLE—
THAT SOME PEOPLE
BELIEVE THIS STUFF

It's absolutely a miracle.

—Jacinto Santacruz, a 26-year-old factory worker who in
2006 discovered a gob of chocolate in a mixing
vat that looked something like the Virgin Mary

They kneel in front of Our Lady of the Underpass.

They pray to Tortilla Jesus.

They give thanks and praise to the Holy Virgin Grilled Cheese Sammich.

They tremble at the image of the Mother Teresa Cinnamon Bun.

They cry, "It's a miracle!" when they see Jesus of Pittsburgh.

They are the thousands upon thousands of true believers who flock to the sites of weeping icons and holy images in strange and mundane places, believing these things to be signs from God.

If they're right, the Almighty has a wicked sense of humor. Hundreds of millions of people are looking for some kind of affirmation from the heavenly above—and he responds by giving us an image of his only son on a Pizza Hut billboard?

◎

April 2005. A grimy underpass of the Kennedy Expressway in Chicago—a dark, damp place where you would normally find nothing more than discarded soda cans and fast-food wrappers, maybe a random shoe or beer bottle, possibly a rodent.

Today, though, this is a holy place. At least a hundred people are queued up behind police barricades, as photographers, TV camera crews, and print journalists stand nearby, taking notes and shooting footage.

Nearby, three squad cars: one from the Chicago Police, one unmarked car with doors open and lights flashing, and one Illinois State Police car.

The people waiting in line are white, black, Hispanic. Wearing gym shoes and casual clothes, holding rosary beads, toting digital cameras, waiting for their moment.

We're all here because there's a stain on the wall that (according to some observers) resembles the Virgin Mary, and somebody noticed it, and somebody else called the media, and now every news organization, from the *Chicago Sun-Times* to the *New Zealand Herald*, is running stories about Our Lady of the Underpass.

We in the media, we love these stories. We love showing the faithful as they keen and tremble, we love focusing on the supposed miracle, and we love putting a little ironic touch on the story, as if to wink at the viewer and say, "Not that we're buying any of this stuff, but miracles *do* happen . . ."

There's a police barricade in front of the Virgin Mary apparition—or as you might call it, the *friggin' oil stain on an underpass*—so you can't get too close. The surrounding semicircle of a shrine includes handmade artwork, pictures of children, flowers, rosaries, holy cards, many flickering candles.

One by one, the faithful approach the shrine, make the sign of the cross, and pray. Some kneel. A few cry.

When it's my turn, I stand and regard the stain. From a certain angle, it bears a passing resemblance to some standard artwork we've all seen depicting the Virgin Mary. From another angle, it looks like an undistinguished blob.

As I noted in a column at the time, there was a homeless guy leaning against a street pole just a block away, holding up a sign that said, "HELP, I'M HUNGRY." I witnessed dozens of people who walked right by the homeless guy on their way to the shrine— walked right past him as if he were invisible. Nobody dropped so much as a quarter in his direction.

If this were my movie, that homeless man would be Jesus in undercover mode—and after an hour or so, he'd walk over and announce himself to the "faithful" lining up to pray at an oil stain, and tell them they're all kinda missing the point.

No matter what you think of religious visions, doesn't it seem like there was at least some *dignity* to the claims of miracles back in the day?

Little girls would claim to have seen apparitions of the Virgin Mary. Men of faith would claim God appeared before them. Towns-folk would flock to the site where a statue of Jesus was said to be weeping.

If there are stories about 19th-century manifestations of the image of Jesus in a loaf of bread or a perfect likeness of the Virgin Mary popping up in a bowl of gruel or on the side of a carriage, I've missed them. Even snake oil salesmen dressed nicely.

These days, we still hear about crying paintings in churches and visions of Jesus in the clouds—but we also get stories of holy images appearing in various food products, on doors and windows, in trees and rock formations. Either God is expanding his palette or people are seeing what they want to see in increasingly silly places.

See if you can pick which one of the following items has not been the subject of a Jesus and/or Mary sighting:

- Tortilla
- Door

- Window
- Grilled cheese sandwich
- Shower stall
- Tree
- Piece of firewood
- Soybean oil tank
- Pizza pan
- Pretzel
- Cinnamon bun
- Wall
- Brick
- Pierogi
- Dental X-ray

Answer: It was a trick question. All of the above items have been said to contain a holy image—and in most cases, some people have bought into the nonsense, er, the miracle, and have made the pilgrimage to pay their respects to the suddenly sacred thingy.

Remember the woman who took a bite out of a grilled cheese sandwich before realizing the browned surface looked like the Virgin Mary?

An online casino paid Florida housewife Diane Duyser some $28,000 for the Holy Virgin Grilled Cheese and set up a traveling publicity tour. (She pocketed another $6,000 for the frying pan that produced the miracle grilled cheese.) Astonishingly, the tour was a hit for a while—not only with the public but with the media, which turned out in droves to take video and photos of the sandwich and to interview Duyser, who seemed to revel in the attention. According to one report in the *Miami Herald*, she even planned to get a tattoo of the sandwich over her right breast at Miami Ink, the tattoo parlor made famous by the reality show of the same name.

But Duyser's moment in the spotlight dimmed after President Bush signed a bill outlawing online gambling in the States—meaning the Web site couldn't sponsor her tour anymore. (And to think some say this was an ineffectual presidency.)

As of this writing, the Holy Virgin Grilled Cheese is in a safe-deposit box, still under the ownership of the online gambling site. Diane Duyser is back to being an anonymous suburban housewife. The ride is over.

Like grilled cheese sandwiches, most of these miracles have a shelf life.

◎

Around the same time Duyser was receding into obscurity, a report out of suburban Chicago said a most unusual image had miraculously appeared in a tree outside a health club—but the image didn't resemble Jesus or the Virgin Mary.

It was the recently deceased mayor of the town.

"Some people in town—including [the mayor's] son . . . say they see the mayor's image in the bark on the tree," reported the Chicago *Daily Herald*.

Donald Stephens, 79, died of cancer in April 2007. He was the only mayor Rosemont had ever known, serving the town for more than a half-century.

When construction started on a health club in town, some suggested an ancient, 50-foot sycamore tree near the site be sacrificed. Though the tree was past its best days, Stephens intervened and saved it.

Now people were saying the late mayor's image had appeared in the very tree he had rescued.

"He's still around here," the mayor's son told the *Daily Herald*. "I'm still on my toes."

The media and some curious townsfolk turned out to examine the image. Some said it bore an indisputable resemblance to Stephens. Others said it looked more like Jesus. Still others scoffed at the notion that the markings looked like anything other than, well, markings on a tree.

You can count me in that last group.

◎

It's easy to chuckle at and discount the zany stories about a dead mayor appearing in a tree or a Virgin Mary appearing on a grilled cheese sandwich. Much more troubling—and in some cases, more difficult to dismiss with a joke—are the claims of genuine and profound miracles involving human beings, especially children.

One of the most famous cases in the last quarter-century was the story of Audrey Marie Santo.

In August 1987, three-year-old Audrey fell into the swimming pool in the backyard of her family's home in Worcester, Massachusetts. She lapsed into a coma, from which she never emerged.

In 1988, Audrey's mother, Linda Santo, raised $8,000 to take her daughter to Medjugorje, the famous shrine in Bosnia-Herzegovina. Linda claimed that Audrey's face appeared in the moon, that Audrey saw an apparition of the Virgin Mary, that Audrey communicated with the Virgin Mary, and that Audrey agreed to become a "victim soul"—someone who takes on the sufferings of humankind. Understand, Audrey was not able to talk or communicate in any way, yet her mother made these claims.

Audrey also went into cardiac arrest in Yugoslavia and came very close to dying. That might have been because it's not the greatest idea to transport a tiny child in a coma across the Atlantic—but Linda Santo said Audrey suffered the heart trauma because she was closest to the largest abortion clinic in the country.

Back home in Massachusetts, Audrey's bedroom was turned into a shrine, filled with religious statues and icons and paintings. She took Holy Communion every day. According to Linda, stigmata appeared on Audrey's hands.

The miracles kept coming. Paintings and statues in the bedroom were constantly dripping "blood" or tears of oil. There were reports of hosts bleeding during the Eucharist. Linda claimed an X-ray of Audrey revealed the silhouette of a small angel near her ovaries. On Good Friday, Audrey was said to appear to endure "the

Passion," writhing in pain "that climaxes at three in the afternoon," as one newspaper report put it.

(As kids in Catholic school, we were told that Christ died at approximately 3 P.M. on Good Friday. Neighborhood legend had it that it almost always stormed on Good Friday afternoon. Of course, even if you believe Jesus died at 3 P.M. on the day known as Good Friday, he didn't die at 3 P.M. Central Time, nor did he die at 3 P.M. Eastern Time, when Audrey supposedly went through these contortions of suffering.)

Audrey became a religious superstar. A steady stream of believers made the pilgrimage to the Santo home—some hoping just to touch her and pray for her, others hoping she could cure what ailed them. At one point the wait to see Audrey was 18 months. For some families, she was bigger than Disney World.

Even some cynical reporters who chronicled Audrey's story seemed impressed by Linda's faith, and at a loss to explain some of the alleged miracles. One of the incidents of a host bleeding was reportedly captured on videotape.

With Linda's permission, the *Washington Post* sent a sample of the "tears" to a lab in Pittsburgh. The sample was found to contain 80 percent corn or soybean oil and 20 percent chicken fat.

A company was formed. It was called Apostolate of a Silent Soul, Inc. You could purchase a number of items, including:

- "The Story of Little Audrey Santo—Two hour video . . . scenes include Audrey's Chapel . . . witness statues and holy pictures weeping oil and blood firsthand." ($20)
- "Little Audrey's Photo" ($2.50)
- "Little Audrey's Rhinestone Cross Pin" ($5)
- "Little Audrey's Magnet—Magnet with Little Audrey's picture for your refrigerator" ($1)
- "Little Audrey's Angel Tack Pin—Everyone dons [sic] their cause by pins. Display your cause by wearing Audrey's pin." ($3)
- "Crucifix—Ten-inch crucifix which has been placed in Little Audrey's room. Hang this crucifix in a prominent place in

your home or office and you will be blessed by Jesus and prayed for by Little Audrey." ($10)

Wow. That's either a bold leap of faith or a mind-numbingly cynical statement. You're telling me that if I buy a crucifix and hang it in my home or office, that poor girl stuck in a coma is going to pray for me? How in God's name do you know that?

According to the "Little Audrey Fact Sheet," Audrey's accident occurred at 11:03 A.M. on August 9, 1987—and the bomb fell at Nagasaki at 11:03 A.M. on August 9, 1945, exactly 42 years earlier. (Again, nobody's taking the whole time zone thing into account, but there you have it.) Why this is significant, the fact sheet doesn't say.

To its credit, the Catholic Church said the true statement of faith in the Audrey Santo case was to be found in the family's belief in God and in their dedication to Audrey. The church noted that paranormal claims are not evidence of miracles and reminded the faithful that one is not supposed to pray "to" anyone except God. If there were prayers to be said in Audrey's presence, they should have been *for* Audrey—not requests for her to perform magical cures from within her coma.

Perhaps those who find images of Mary and Jesus in potato chips and bowls of guacamole truly believe they've experienced a miracle. Perhaps they see the images and figure it's probably a coincidence, but if they can make a few bucks and remind others of God's message, where's the harm in that?

It's the Linda Santos of the world that create a more serious dilemma. There are documented cases of fakery—people faking miracles by manufacturing weeping icons and other miraculous occurrences. Nobody ever proved that Linda Santo or anyone else around little Audrey executed such ongoing, complicated parlor tricks as making stigmata appear or causing icons to weep. Then again, there's no concrete evidence to back up the claims about

Audrey communicating with the Virgin Mary and performing miracles from her bed.

Was there a conspiracy among Audrey's family and friends to create the miracle of this little girl? That's almost as difficult to fathom as the notion that all these magical occurrences actually took place. That the mother of a little girl in a coma would exploit that child for so many years—what kind of soulless monster would do that?

It's entirely possible Linda Santo believes all her claims with 100 percent of her being. That doesn't mean that these things all happened the way she says they happened or that there's any concrete proof of any true miracle surrounding her little girl.

But as Penn Jillette pointed out in an episode of *Bullshit!* that addressed some of these miracles, whether you're a middle-aged woman grilling up a cheese sandwich or a mother suffering the terrible tragedy of her little girl disappearing into a coma after a preventable accident, if you can somehow attach yourself to a miracle, you become important, and then the outside world will care about you and pay attention to you, and you won't seem so alone. The allure of that cannot be underestimated.

Audrey Santo died of respiratory failure on April 17, 2007. One could probably find some sort of historical connection to the time and date of her death. Or one could simply offer heartfelt prayers that she found eternal peace.

VII

THE CULTURE

20

THE "WAR" ON CHRISTMAS

More than 90 percent of American homes celebrate Christmas. But the small minority that is trying to impose its will on the majority is so vicious, so dishonest—and it has to be dealt with.

> —Bill O'Reilly addressing the war on Christmas on his syndicated radio show, December 9, 2004, as reported by Media Matters for America

Christmas comes to my hometown—and yours—every year, usually about four days after Halloween. Even as the last pumpkins are removed from front porches, and the bags of candy corn and miniature candy bars and apple-flavored bubble gum and other tooth-rotting delights go on sale at half-price, and the cards wishing loved ones a "Spook-tacular Halloween!" are tucked away in memory boxes, stores put up their Christmas decorations, local "Lite FM" stations shift into 24-hour holiday tune mode (love that "Jingle Bell Rock," just can't get enough!), and Sunday newspapers start to bulge with ads for Christmas sales.

For a full two months—one-sixth of the calendar year—the United States of America is knee-deep in Christmas cheer. Everywhere you look, you see bright lights and ornament-spangled wreaths, and myriad images of the baby Jesus, Mary, Joseph, the Three Wise Men, and other important New Testament figures such as Santa Claus and Rudolph and Winky the Slightly Drunk Elf, who has loads of bargains for you at your local home improvement store. By my unofficial count—and by *unofficial*, I mean I'm inventing this figure, but if anything it's probably a little low—there are approximately 874 billion-kajillion decorations, signs, lights, songs, trees, and ceremonies celebrating Christmas by name in this country, every year.

There are also hundreds of thousands of churches, where you are free to worship and to pray.

But don't let those superficial indicators fool you. The truth is, the secular media and the godless merchants have been conspiring for years to eliminate any religious references to the holiday season, and if we're not diligent, it won't be long before Christmas disappears altogether.

Haven't you heard? There's a war on Christmas, *and the heathens are winning!*

Just ask Bill O'Reilly. Each year around the holidays, the most popular and powerful talk show host in all of cable television dedicates an inordinate percentage of his programming to waging a heroic fight against the heathens who are trying to Grinch this country straight to hell.

Or John Gibson, another Fox News warlord who penned a book titled *The War on Christmas: How the Liberal Plot to Ban the Sacred Christian Holiday Is Worse Than You Thought*, one of my favorite conservative-themed book titles of all time. (It's right up there with Ann Coulter's latest, *Kill Them All!: My Plan to Wipe All the Godless, Serial-Killing, Baby-Eating Liberals from the Face of the Earth Before I Turn 50, Which Is Sooner Than You Think.*)

Or the late televangelist Jerry Falwell, who in 2005 ran a "Friend or Foe Christmas Campaign."

Or the Alliance Defense Fund, which runs a campaign called "Merry Christmas: It's okay to say it." And here I'd been avoiding the phrase for years, for fear of arrest.

Or organizations such as the Catholic League and the American Family Association, which spend a good deal of time and effort going after the liberal media and those who believe in the separation of church and state, apparently because they've already solved such nagging problems as starvation, poverty, abandoned children, and other issues that should bother us more than, say, whether people say "Merry Christmas!" or "Happy Holidays!" when greeting one another in a big-box department store.

◎

Like the so-called epidemics of shark attacks and child kidnappings from summers gone by (remember?), "the war on Christmas" is a non-story created by certain segments of the media in an effort to generate controversy and increase ratings.

It's a perfect go-to issue for some conservative commentators and columnists and their fans. These folks are laughably—or should I say sadly—eager to believe we live a world in which millions of Jesus-hating Stalinists are engaging in a vast, nationwide conspiracy to take the "Christ" out of all things Christmas. It provides a perfect outlet for all that antiliberal vitriol. Who better to hate than the godless, Satan-friendly heathens who are attacking the baby Jesus?

Even if it's all just a load of overhyped crapola.

There's been talk of a war against Christmas for decades, but only in recent years has it become a perennial cause among conservatives.

In winter 2005, spurred on by a few isolated incidents and misreported events, conservative hysterics went into full Chicken Little mode and claimed Christmas was becoming an endangered species.

Leading the charges against the forces of evil: the great and all-powerful Bill O'Reilly.

As I once said in a *Chicago Sun-Times* column, O'Reilly is the most skilled and successful propagandist on television and radio today. He somehow keeps a straight face as he proclaims his show a "No-Spin Zone," when in reality all he does is spin the facts to his own agenda. He's got more spin moves than Allen Iverson in a game of one-on-one. (Once when I appeared as a phone-in guest on O'Reilly's radio program to talk about the war on Christmas, I was put on hold as O'Reilly started ranting about the elitist, mainstream media. Later, as Bill and I engaged in some good-natured bantering—he's always been fair to me on television and on the radio and has given me room to make my points—he challenged me to come up with "one example" when he's ever spun the truth. "You just did it a few minutes ago when you talked about the elitist media and painted yourself as an outsider," I replied. "You've got the most successful talk show on cable television, a nationally syndicated radio show, a nationally syndicated newspaper column, bestselling books, a Web site where you sell *Factor* merchandise. You make tens of millions of dollars a year. You *are* the elite media!" He didn't really disagree with that, mainly because it's the truth.)

O'Reilly is filled with holy anger, unleashing his fury on stores that dare to have their employees say "Happy Holidays!" instead of "Merry Christmas." Also incurring his wrath are any media outlets that have the temerity to publish writings by those who say the war on Christmas is, you know, bullshit.

"I am not going to let oppressive, totalitarian, anti-Christian forces in his country diminish and denigrate the holiday and the celebration," said O'Reilly. "I am not going to let it happen. I'm gonna use all the power that I have on radio and television to bring horror into the world of people who are trying to do that."

Wow, just like Jesus would do!

Let's take a closer look at just a few of the examples cited by conservatives as evidence of a widespread war on Christmas.

William Donahue of the Catholic League for Religious and Civil Rights and other right-wing groups protested that the official 2005 White House holiday card was too generic. The card from George and Laura Bush, which was mailed to 1.5 million of their closest friends, had cover art of the two presidential dogs and the presidential cat roaming on the White House lawn. The greeting: "Best Wishes for the Holiday Season."

Joseph Farah, editor of the conservative Web site WorldNet-Daily.com, told the *Washington Post*, "Bush claims to be a born-again, evangelical Christian. But he sure doesn't act like one. I threw out my White House card as soon as I got it."

I guess Farah was hoping the Bushes would use artwork from *A Charlie Brown Christmas*.

Donahue, a blustery, camera-loving blowhard who can always be counted on to deliver sound bites of outrage whenever there's a religion-related news issue, told ABC News: "At a time when a lot of Christians today are very upset about the way our society is dumbing down Christmas, they certainly don't want the president of the United States chiming in. We know he is a man of courage, so why is he giving in to the forces of political correctness?"

Damn, how did Donahue hear about the secret meetings of the Politically Correct Police, at which we outlined our plans to push our agenda on the world by forcing the president of the United States to send out generic holiday cards?

More from Donahue: "Prior to Clinton, none of the presidents had a problem saying 'Christmas' at Christmastime. Now Bush is pulling a Clinton. I expected more from this guy."

Is it too much to expect Donahue to be a little more histori-cally accurate when appearing on a national newscast? Let's go back to 1955, when the official "Christmas" card from the White House read "Season's Greetings," with no written or visual refer-ence to Christmas.

Of course, that famous liberal Dwight D. Eisenhower was pres-ident in 1955, and we all know he was a godless Communist, right?

Other conservative leaders got all worked up when city leaders in Boston referred to its beautiful, festively decorated, 50-foot spruce as a "holiday tree." The Reverend Jerry Falwell threatened a mas-sive lawsuit, which would be pretty funny if it wasn't so sad and delusional. ("Ladies and gentlemen of the jury, I implore you. Take a look at Exhibit A, and tell me that's anything *but* a Christmas tree!") The mayor of Boston, sensing an opportunity for the easiest holiday-themed public relations victory since the judge ruled in favor of Kris Kringle as the true Santa Claus in *Miracle on 34th Street*, called a press conference and boldly declared, "It'll be a Christmas tree as long as I'm around."

Does is it really matter to actual Christians if their city's ginormous tree is called a Christmas tree or a holiday tree? How many references to Christmas trees can one find in the New Testament, anyway?

The so-called Christmas tree is a cutesy touch that's been added to our list of holiday traditions only in recent decades—and we stole the practice from pagan winter solstice rituals. Politicians and civic leaders that crusade for the Christmas tree might as well be defending the sacred rights of the Easter bunny and the St. Patrick's Day leprechaun.

It's all cartoon stuff, folks, and it has nothing to do with the birth of the baby Jesus.

One of O'Reilly's pet causes was a story out of Dodgeville, Wisconsin, where a teacher allegedly changed the lyrics of "Silent Night," turning it into a Jesus-free song about the weather.

"People are outraged!" said O'Reilly in December 2005. "We sent a demand letter asking them to immediately change the song and allow the actual lyrics of 'Silent Night,' and if they do not, if they insist on this ridiculous course of action, we'll file a federal lawsuit."

Again with the threat of a lawsuit. I thought conservatives were supposed to be *against* clogging up our courtrooms with frivolous actions.

First, is this really how you'd wage a war on Christmas—by having an elementary school teacher in Cheeseland alter the lyrics to "Silent Night" for a school play? With volleys like that, it would take only about 137,000 years to win this so-called war and erase Jesus from the equation.

One other problem with this example: it's literally true, but it's not *accurate*.

Nobody at Ridgewood Elementary changed the lyrics to "Silent Night." They were simply staging a play called *The Little Tree's Christmas Gift*, a play about a Charlie Brown–esque Christmas tree that sits on the lot, unsold. In the play, the lyrics to "Silent Night" *are changed to reflect the sorry state of the tree*: "Cold in the night, no one in sight, winter winds, swirl and bite . . ."

See, people do that with songs sometimes. They take a popular melody and put in some words, for effect. For example, the music for the "Star-Spangled Banner" was originally from an English drinking tune called "The Anacreontic Song."

As the Think Progress Web site (http://thinkprogress.org) reported, the author of *The Little Tree's Christmas Gift* (note that it's not "The Little Tree's *Holiday* Gift") is one Dwight Elrich, who leads the New Covenant Singers of Bel Air Presbyterian Church in Los Angeles. The play, which has been performed in a number of churches across the country, closes with a cast-and-audience sing-along of "We Wish You a Merry Christmas."

Yeah, that Elrich guy sounds like a real atheist waging a bloody fight against the Christmas holiday.

On another program in December 2005, O'Reilly told his 2.5-plus million viewers about a township in Michigan that "opposes red and green clothing on anyone . . . they basically said . . . 'We don't want you wearing red or green.' I would dress up from head to toe in red to green if I were in Saginaw, Michigan."

Well, I'd *walk* to Saginaw just to see Big Bill dressed in red and green from head to toe—but as Saginaw TV station WNEM-5 reported, the whole red-and-green story simply isn't true.

Also not true: O'Reilly's claim that a school in Plano, Texas, had enacted a similar ban.

O'Reilly, on December 9, 2005: "In Plano, Texas, a school told students they couldn't wear red and green because they are Christmas colors."

Dr. Doug Otto, the superintendent of schools for that district: "The school district does not restrict students or staff from wearing certain color clothes during holiday times or any other school days."

As specious or thin as some of O'Reilly examples might be, at least he didn't dedicate an entire book to the utterly phony notion that seculars are waging a war on Christmas. O'Reilly's colleague John Gibson did just that—and the result is one of the most fundamentally unsound and unintentionally funny books ever written about the so-called culture wars.

The subtitle to *The War on Christmas* implies that Gibson is going to explain to us *How the Liberal Plot to Ban the Sacred Christian Holiday Is Worse Than You Thought*. In just 15 words, three points are made:

1. Make no mistake about it: there *is* a liberal plot against Christmas.
2. Gibson assumes that you, the reader, think this plot is "bad."
3. *It's worse than you thought!*

The cover artwork depicts a hand yanking on the electrical cord of a brightly decorated Christmas tree. On the back cover, the poor little Christmas tree has been left on its side, with broken ornament shards scattered about. Other than the angel figurine atop the tree, there's not even a whisper of anything truly religious. If there's a true war on Christmas, why not put the baby Jesus on your book's cover?

In the introduction, Gibson cites a few isolated examples of political correctness run amok—for example, a New Hampshire junior high school student who reportedly was banned from a dance because he was dressed as Santa—and makes the claim that "almost everywhere a school district is limiting what Christmas carols kids can sing or hear, or a district is considering it. Almost everywhere a school district has decided that kids cannot have Christmas parties . . . almost everywhere school districts have either disinvited Santa or are giving him sidelong glances of suspicion."

Ooh, he knows about our sidelong glances of suspicion! I knew we should have been subtle.

But really: This stuff is happening "almost everywhere"?

Gibson then asks, "Whose fault is this? Well, for those who like to jump to conclusions, no, it's not just liberal Jews. I should state for the record that my Jewish son helped me research this book because he agrees that the war on Christmas has gone too far."

Yes, and I'll bet some of your best friends are Jews, too. But hey, thanks for bringing up that whole liberal-Jew thing just so you could shoot it down.

Gibson's "evidence" of the widespread liberal war consists of a grand total of seven primary incidents in towns such as Mustang, Oklahoma, and Maplewood, New Jersey.

In the year 2000 in Covington, Georgia, we're told, the Newton County School Board received a letter saying that the American Civil Liberties Union would pursue legal action if the board continued to use the word *Christmas* on the school calendar.

The bastards! Will they stop at nothing?

Another chapter is devoted to the controversy in Baldwin City, Kansas, where "Santa Claus was banned from the Baldwin City schools," as Gibson puts it. The firestorm started when a man playing Santa Claus—an assistant minister at a local church—reportedly told a class of kindergarten students, "If you believe in Jesus, Santa will bring you toys." There was a debate about whether the man actually preached in such a manner—he denied doing so—but there was concern that "Santa" was proselytizing religion when he should have been just handing out candy canes and saying "Ho ho ho."

Gibson's other examples are similar in scope and in silliness. Some minor debate gets turned into a full-blown (albeit local) controversy, with advocates on both sides getting all worked up over issues that could have been resolved with everyone taking a deep breath and invoking healthy measures of common sense.

But where are the stories of liberals trying to "ban the sacred Christian holiday"? We get isolated tales of individuals and organizations trying to ban the word *Christmas* or symbols of the holiday from certain activities or public places—but no evidence that anyone is trying to ban the holiday itself, which of course would be about as futile as trying to ban tomorrow's sunrise.

One assumes Gibson selected episodes in places such as Eugene, Oregon, and Indianapolis to illustrate the far reaches of the liberal plot. But if the liberals are trying to get rid of Christmas, why aren't they concentrating on the major markets? An overzealous parent here, an overreaching ACLU attorney there—in what universe does that constitute a conspiracy against Christmas?

Gibson's own book is the best evidence that there is no such conspiracy. If these are the best examples he can provide, the sacred Christian holiday has never been more secure.

I am a Christian.

I was raised Catholic by parents who haven't missed a Sunday at church for a half-century. (My track record isn't nearly as impressive, but the walls do not shake and crumble when I enter houses of worship.) For eight years, I attended St. Jude the Apostle in South Holland, Illinois.

I know the Bible. I believe in God.

I am not shy about expressing my beliefs in superficial ways. There's a Celtic cross tattooed on my forearm, and I wear a crucifix around my neck. At Christmastime, my house is adorned with decorations, including a tree, lights, and the biggest mistletoe money can buy.

If there really were a war on Christmas, I'd be on the side of Christmas.

But there isn't.

Good Lord (so to speak), this is a country *dripping* in Christmas. If 50 percent of all the Christmas decorations, displays, musicals, plays, parties, and celebrations were wiped from existence next December, we'd still be overwhelmed by the sheer volume of Christmas-mania from coast to coast.

I'm not saying there haven't been a few isolated incidents over the years involving some ridiculous attempt to make Christmas more generic, whether it's some company president telling employees not to say "Merry Christmas!" in the workplace, or a moronic teacher telling a class of first-graders that Santa Claus is a myth and Jesus wasn't really born on December 25.

But how exactly does that translate to a friggin' *war* on Christmas?

The United States is an overwhelmingly Christian nation. The idea that some kid in a department store saying "Season's Greetings!" instead of "Merry Christmas" constitutes an attack on the holiday is beyond silly and is an insult to true Christians.

21

CLASSICAL GAS

Don't buy gas if you don't need it.

—President George W. Bush, offering advice on how
consumers can cope with the rising price
of gasoline, August 2005

Sometimes you just have to envy George Bush's worldview. It's so, what's the word . . . *basic.*

With gas prices escalating in late summer 2005, Bush uttered the first thought that popped into his head: If you don't need gas, don't buy it! And hey, if you don't want it to rain, think sunny thoughts.

After all, the president gets around just fine every day, whether it's via motorcade or helicopter or *Air Force One,* and he probably couldn't even remember the last time *he* needed gas. If the president of the United States can travel without buying gasoline every darn week, why can't others follow his example?

See, the tricky thing about gasoline is, we need it to make our cars go. Even the most fuel-efficient vehicles don't actually work without fuel.

Of course, there's a difference between the working-class family with a hybrid car used mostly for trips to work and school, and the cigar-chomping fathead who takes his Hummer with the "GASEATER" license plates to the end of the driveway to pick up the morning newspaper. If we all banded together as a nation and decided to cut back our driving even 10 percent—taking the bicycle to work once a week, walking to the corner store, stuff like that—we could probably put a real dent in gas prices and help save the environment.

And the chances of that happening are about the same as the chances that one day George Bush will flap his arms and fly instead of taking *Air Force One*.

We all know it would be cheaper and more environment friendly to drive fuel-efficient cars, to use public transportation instead of driving to work every day, to carpool, to cut down on unnecessary driving. We all agree these are great ideas.

For other people.

Do you know anyone who carpools? How many people really want to share a ride to work every day with the neighbor or the coworker who lives in the neighborhood?

I think it's great when Hollywood superstars leave their 7,000-square-foot mansions that have been carved into formerly pristine mountains and drive to movie premieres in their Toyota Priuses and Honda Civics, leaving the Bentley and the Humvee and the Navigator and the Porsche Cayenne back in the garage. It shows that some celebrities aren't just talking the talk when it comes to fuel efficiency—they're walking the walk. (Or is that driving the drive?)

Me? Sorry, but I just can't embrace the Corolla or the Aveo. I drive a late-model Mach 5, a real-life version of the car favored by Speed Racer back in the day. It gets approximately two city blocks to the gallon.

In summer 2007, gas prices were so ridiculous in downtown Chicago that when you inserted your credit card into the slot, they asked for your zip code. Why? Because in all likelihood, your purchase was going to exceed $50, and they wanted to make sure you weren't using a stolen credit card. Gasoline was like liquid gold.

Consumers, of course, were fed up. We knew this because every local newscast in the country featured interviews with motorists who were filling up. Inevitably they'd say, "I'm fed up."

And then they'd go back to filling up.

Nevertheless, there was the feeling that something had to be done. We had to let the government and Big Oil know that we were mad as hell and we weren't going to take it anymore!

It was time for another Great American Gas-Out.

We'd been down this road before. In 1999, in 2000, in 2003, in 2005. Each time, the e-mail was pretty much the same:

DO NOT PUMP GAS ON MAY 15TH!!!

It has been calculated that if everyone in the United States didn't purchase a drop of gasoline for one day, the oil companies would choke on their stockpiles. At the same time it would hit the industry with a net loss of nearly $5 billion....

We can make a difference. If you want to help, just send this to everyone you know and ask them to do the same. WE CAN MAKE A DIFFERENCE!!!

Remember the time-honored rule of urban legends and conspiracy theories: JUST BECAUSE YOU USE ALL CAPS AND ADD MULTIPLE EXCLAMATION POINTS DOESN'T MAKE IT TRUE!!!!!!!

All e-mail boycott campaigns have one thing in common. They don't work.

Giving up gasoline for one day, only to fill your tank later in the week, makes about as much sense as giving up drinking for one day, only to belly up to the bar a day later. There's a reason Big Oil is called Big Oil; it's, you know, *big*. Even if they rang up a grand total of $0 on one day, so what? They'd make it up the next day, when everyone returned to the pumps.

The gas-outs are never about reducing gasoline consumption. It's always about taking a single day off from buying gas. Such a movement wouldn't result in a net loss of $4.60, let alone $4.6 billion.

In 1999 a Los Angeles city councilman officially urged residents to participate in a one-day gas-out. Virtually nobody listened.

By 2007 we were seeing headlines like this one from the Web site of the NBC affiliate in Cincinnati:

"Economic Expert Says May 15 Gas Boycott Will Prove Useless."

Exactly.

My favorite failed boycott story of the 21st century: Bill O'Reilly's four-year moratorium on French services and products.

In March 2003, O'Reilly called for a boycott of all things French, in response to President Jacques Chirac's refusal to support the American military effort in Iraq. Over the next four years, O'Reilly would make the claim that the boycott was costing the French hundreds of millions of dollars—but the reality is that American consumption of French goods and services *increased* in most significant categories, including wine, confectionary products, baked goods, and plastic materials.

22

WARNING: JAGER BOMBS CAN KILL YOU!

I stopped drinking Jager in high school.

—Vincent Chase's best friend and manager, "E," turning down Seth Green's offer to buy the boys a round of Jager shots on an episode of *Entourage*

On a Saturday night in spring 2007, I found myself at a bar called Legends, in the Caesars casino and hotel complex in Elizabeth, Indiana.

Yes, there is a Caesars, complete with Roman Empire imagery and sanctioned games of chance, in a small town in deep southern Indiana, just a stone's throw north of Kentucky. (Some people call this region "Kentuckiana." It's a much better name than "Indyucky.") There's even a sorta Roman-sounding recorded voice greeting when you reach the end of the people movers for folks who find it too much of a strain to walk from the hotel to the casino:

"Global citizens!" bellows the faux-Roman voice. "You are now reaching the end of the moving walkway."

I guess that's for the people who find it too difficult to look down and notice that the rubberized, motorized footing beneath them is giving way to, you know, carpeting.

Anyway. I was at Caesars for a number of World Series of Poker tour events, and after a long day of playing Texas Hold'em, I met up with some friends at the Legends bar, which is decorated with weird, abstract paintings of legendary entertainers such as Sammy Davis Jr., Michael Jordan, and Elvis, who all looked as if they had been in serious car accidents. The entertainment consisted of a local band that covered songs by the likes of Tommy Tutone, John Mellencamp, and the Beatles—somehow making all those tunes sound alike—and a talented bar staff that would occasionally pause from their drink-serving duties to demonstrate their abilities to juggle flaming tiki torches.

So it was pretty much like Vegas during the Rat Pack heyday.

In order to celebrate our magical getaway, our group decided to order up some shots.

"Six Jager Bombs!" was the rallying cry from one of my buddies.

Little did we know we were flirting with possible instantaneous death!

Jagermeister is a popular, mysterious, and fairly disgusting spirit— a dark, black-licorice-flavored, icy cold drink with a 70-proof jolt. In certain bars across the country, you'll see those special Jagermeister machines, keeping the concoction chilled to a frigid five degrees.

Urban legend has it that Jagermeister contains elk's blood or deer's blood—witness the bloody, dark color of the liquor and the stag's head logo on the bottle—but since most of us aren't vampires and we'd find that a bit nauseating, the truth is a bit more mundane. There are 56 herbs, roots, and spices in Jager, including some "secret spices," according to the company, which is based in Germany.

Jager has been popular in the United States since the 1970s. I remember Spring Breakers doing shots of Jager back in the days when the Police and the Clash were burning up the music charts. To this day, it remains the go-to drink of choice for a number of heavy metal bands and is also used as a prop to indicate a certain kind of, shall we say, straightforward and unsophisticated brand of partying, on TV shows such as *Scrubs*, *The Office*, and *How I Met Your Mother*.

In *Scary Movie 3*, Ajay Naidu says, "If only I hadn't fallen asleep while driving for that exact 20 minutes. If only I hadn't drank that whole bottle of Jagermeister. If only I hadn't killed that hooker."

You get the idea. That bit wouldn't really work if you substituted "1993 Dom Pérignon" for "Jagermeister."

In recent years, Jager has enjoyed a huge surge in popularity, thanks in no small part to the popularity of the so-called Jager Bomb—a potent combination of Jager and Red Bull (or Monster or Rock Star or some other energy drink).

First you pour the Red Bull into a tall glass. Then you drop a shot glass filled with Jagermeister into the tall glass and drink the concoction as fast as possible. (Or you can just mix the two together, creating a Jager Blaster.)

Then you announce your candidacy for governor.

Or you say "Whooooo!" as you slam the glass down and congratulate yourself on attaining a certain level of maturity that comes only with age and experience and spiritual enlightenment.

Across the country, Jager rules.

"If you're looking to get messed up, that's the way to go," says a bartender in an article in the *Great Falls (Montana) Tribune*.

"I even bought a Jager machine, but my fiancée doesn't want to keep it in the house," says a guy in an article in the *Charlotte Observer*.

"Jager Bombs Changed My Life," reads a T-shirt available from CafePress.com.

But here's the thing about those Jager Bombs—they can kill you.

Or so the story goes.

Every generation has its urban legend warning stories about some drug or drink or wacky junk food concoction that can kill you or create some sort of amazing reaction.

In the 1960s there were stories about kids dropping LSD and then staring at the sun until they went blind.

In the 1970s we heard that Mikey from the Life Cereal commercials had died from ingesting the carbonated candy Pop Rocks and washing it down with a can of Coca-Cola, causing his stomach to explode.

In the 1990s we were told that Altoids mints could enhance oral sex. (Monica Lewinsky and President Bill even tested that theory, so the story goes.)

In the new millennium the story was that mixing Mentos mints with Diet Coke could kill you.

Another story said you could create impressive geysers known as "Mentos eruptions" by mixing Mentos with Diet Coke. Turns out that one was true. And if you mix Pop Rocks, Altoids, *and* Mentos with Coca-Cola, you'll suddenly have the ability to sing just like James Blunt. *"You're beautiful . . ."* Amazing.

As for the Jager Bombs: in 2006, stories started circulating about the supposed dangers in drinking such a potent mix of booze and energy drink.

"Be careful with those Jager Bombs, especially if you're over 30!" said an e-mail I received one day.

"If you down even a single Jager Bomb very quickly and you have a heart condition or you're not in the shape you used to be, just that one Jager Bomb can cause your heart to explode, killing you instantly!"

In an article syndicated to numerous newspapers in early 2007, journalist Misty Harris wrote, "Did you hear the one about the guy whose heart exploded after he drank a Jager Bomb? How about the girl who was 'date-raped' with the trendy nightclub drink, or the man who took a single gulp and went into cardiac arrest?"

Harris quotes a Canadian man who said he tried to buy a round of Jager Bombs for his "time-weathered friends," only to have the bartender refuse to make them because of liability concerns. The owner of the bar confirmed to Harris that he was no longer serving Jager Bombs to customers: "We don't want to have any problems."

Presumably this establishment also bans the Diet Coke/Mentos combination, not to mention Pop Rocks and Coca-Cola.

As you might expect, medical experts say there's no danger of a healthy person dropping dead from downing Jager Bombs—unless, of course, you drink 86 of them in one night.

At which point your heart will leap out of your chest and fly higher than a Mentos eruption as you collapse to the floor in an alcoholic heap of wasted life.

Good times.

23

THE GODLESS
DOLLAR COIN

*By omitting these words, our politically correct, secularist
leaders made a conscientious [sic] decision that either
God does not exist, or that God exists, but can no longer
be trusted.*

—Online rant about the new "Godless" dollar coin

Quick!

Check your pockets and the change dish on your dresser right
now and riddle me this: how many dollar coins do you have on you
right now?

Take your time while counting. I'll wait.

Now, using my amazing powers of psychic deduction, I am
going to ascertain the exact number of dollar coins in your
possession.

Zero.

How'd I do? Thank you, thank you very much, you're too kind.

I'll bet more than 90 percent of you have absolutely no dollar
coins on you at this moment.

Our pockets and purses are already filled with wallets and cell
phones and iPhones and Blackberrys and keys and quarters and

nickels and dimes and those nearly worthless pennies. The last thing we want is another heavy coin in the mix.

This is thing about Americans: we hate the dollar coin. We hated the Susan B. Anthony dollar and we never liked the Sacagawea dollar, and to date I've seen little evidence of any national fondness for the presidential dollar coins, introduced to the mix in early 2007.

The dollar bill wears out much faster than the dollar coin. The dollar coin comes in handy when you're feeding parking meters and laundry machines and vending machines (if such machines are equipped to accept the $1 coin). But we don't care. Other nations use $1 and $2 coins, but we don't like 'em. We'll embrace the dollar coin right around the same time we throw our arms around the metric system.

Yet the government keeps trying—so in February 2007 the first presidential dollar coins entered circulation.

I'm writing this entry in early 2008, and I'm not exaggerating for effect when I say I have yet to encounter one presidential dollar in any setting, from stores to casinos to taxicabs to coffee shops to looking down and finding a shiny new dollar on the street.

Even though the first presidential dollar coins hardly inspired a frenzy of excitement ("This Washington dollar is cool, but I really can't wait for the John Adams edition!"), they did inspire an almost instant conspiracy theory.

Did you hear? "They" are keeping God's name off the new dollar coin.

You may have received an e-mail like this one:

New Dollar Bill Unveiled, and You Guessed It—"IN GOD WE TRUST" IS GONE!!!!!

If ever there was a reason to boycott something, THIS IS IT!!!!

The words "In God We Trust" are nowhere to be found on the new presidential coins. This is an outrage!

Do not accept the new dollar coins as change.
Together we can force them out of circulation. Please send to all on your email list!!!

DO YOU KNOW ANYONE—sorry, had to get out of "caps lock" mode there—Do you know anyone who writes like that in real life? If you do, buy that person a pound of decaf, an aromatherapy candle, and some bath suds, and tell him or her to take the day off and relax.

According to the conspiracy theorists, the U.S. Mint had caved to pressure from the liberal left and the ACLU and had decided not to inscribe *In God We Trust* anywhere on the new dollar coins.

Sure enough, not long after the coins entered circulation, there were literally thousands of reports of the "Godless" coins and photos of them all over the Internet. Of course, simple home computer technology makes it pretty easy to erase a slogan or add the face of, say, Simon Cowell to a dollar coin—but what about all those eyewitness reports from people claiming to have possession of the Godless coins?

Turns out that at least 50,000 presidential dollars *were* minted without the *In God We Trust* inscription, but it was due to a manufacturing error at the Philadelphia Mint. (The Philadelphia Mint—weren't they a U.S. women's tennis team in the 1970s?)

For the first time in 70 years, the U.S. Mint had decided to place inscriptions on the edge of a coin—the presidential dollar. With new machines required and approximately 300 million presidential coins minted, some kind of problem was almost inevitable.

Owing to some sort of production error, the phrases *In God We Trust* and *E Pluribus Unum* (which, of course, means "Do I Look Fat In This?") weren't inscribed on the edges of a large batch of coins out of the Philadelphia Mint, thus giving rise to the talk of a conspiracy to remove God's name from official U.S. coinage.

In fact, there is a law requiring that *In God We Trust* and *E Pluribus* be inscribed on all U.S. currency, and there is no movement afoot to change this law. (The Limbaughs and O'Reillys and Hannitys of the world would bury any politician foolish enough to take on this seemingly insignificant issue.)

Opportunistic types flooded eBay with offers to sell the "rare" Godless coins, usually for about $10. There were also reports of people trying to file down the inscriptions on dollar coins in an effort to pass them off as the flawed version.

"The edge lettering on some perfectly made coins is being intentionally removed in machine shops to fraudulently make the coins appear to have a plain edge without the date, without the mint mark and without the mottoes," a coin expert told the *Newark Star-Ledger* in April 2007. "You run the risk of paying $100 or more for an altered coin that's only worth $1."

As cons go, filing down a dollar coin doesn't exactly rank with Newman and Redford's endgame shootout in *The Sting*, does it?

Although even that's a bit more sophisticated than some of the stuff you see people trying to pull on eBay. As I browsed the site looking for flawed presidential coins, I came across a listing for a "set" of two mint-condition, "In God We Trust," standard-issue, George Washington dollar coins, with a "Buy It Now!" price of just $4.25.

Why, that's just a little over the actual value of the two $1 coins, which would be, um, I know . . .

Two dollars.

24

ROCK ME NOSTRADAMUS

Recently I saw a movie on cable TV called "The Man Who Saw Tomorrow," about . . . Nostradamus the prognosticator. . . . Nostradamus claims that first Halley's comet will screw up the entire world and then in the 1990s a Middle East/Russia collaboration will wage nuclear war on the West for 27 years, after which the U.S. and Russia will join together to defeat the Islamic horde. Should I begin to say my prayers?

—From a 1984 question to Cecil Adams of *The Straight Dope*

Wow! That's exactly how it all went down!

Well. Almost.

The most famous prognosticator since biblical times is Michel de Nostredame, aka Nostradamus, the 16th-century French physician/astrologer/author. Nostradamus claimed to be able to see the future, and he wrote hundreds and hundreds of prophecies encased in four-line verses, or quatrains.

Every time there's a modern-day disaster or tragedy, someone trots out some obscure Nostradamus quatrain as "proof" that old Nosty saw it coming.

One of the most famous examples is the supposed prediction of Hitler's reign:

> Beasts ferocious with hunger will cross the rivers
> The greater part of the battlefield will be against Hister
> Into a cage of iron will the great ones be drawn
> When the child of Germany observes nothing

Hister is obviously a reference to Hitler, right? Well, no. It's actually an old name for the lower portion of the Danube, and it appears in dozens of other quatrains by Nostradamus.

The rest is just vaguely worded, semi-intelligible gibberish that could be retrofitted to mean *something* about World War II—if that's what you're looking for.

Such is the case with virtually every single one of Nosty's 900-plus "prophecies." You can take a generic phrase here or a coincidental reference there, apply it to a modern-day tragedy, and say, "See? Nostradamus was a genius!"

In the aftermath of 9/11, a widely circulated e-mail credited Nostradamus with predicting the attacks. He supposedly wrote:

> In the City of God there will be a great thunder
> Two Brothers torn apart by Chaos
> While the fortress endures, the great leader will succumb
> The third big war will begin when the big city is burning

Problem is, Nostradamus didn't pen those lines. In fact, a Canadian university student named Neil Marshall wrote the first three lines a few years prior to 9/11 in an effort to debunk the Nostradamus myth. He couldn't have possibly known that his very lines would be attributed to Nostradamus just a few years later.

Or could he?

Perhaps Neil Marshall is Nostradamus reincarnated!

◎

When John F. Kennedy Jr.'s plane crashed in 1999, some Nostradamus believers pointed to these lines:

> The year 1999 seven months
> From the sky will come the great King of Terror
> To resuscitate the great king of the Mongols

John F. Kennedy Jr., his wife, and his wife's sister were killed when Kennedy's small plane crashed on July 18, 1999. One of Nostradamus's quatrains mentioned "the year 1999 seven months."

End of "eerie similarities." Even if you want to stretch things to the point where death is "the King of Terror," what's up with that whole "king of the Mongols" thing? At the time of John Jr.'s death, he wasn't even king of the magazine world.

And nobody was resuscitated.

Ooh, how about this one:

> From the human flock nine will be sent away
> Separated from their judgment and counsel
> Their fate will be sealed on departure
> Kappa, Thita, Lambda the banished dead err

This is clearly a reference to the *Challenger* space shuttle tragedy of 1986. Clearly. Even though there were seven aboard the *Challenger*—not nine—and the rest of it doesn't mean anything.

And so it goes.

Nostradamus was a kooky guy with a big beard and an active brain and delusions of grandeur. He wrote in vague terms about all manner of future (and past) disasters, wars, and tragedies. When translated, retrofitted, and viewed through the prism of the willing, some of his writings can be connected in the most tenuous terms to real-life events.

If you sat down and wrote nearly a thousand similarly worded quatrains right now, in about 400 years your track record would probably come close to matching Nosty's.

But everyone in your life would abandon you because of the whole "writing a thousand quatrains to prove a point" thing. So don't do it.

VIII

POLITICS

25

BUSH'S MYSTERY BULGE

There are photographs of President Bush from the first debate and he's got some kind of lump in the back of his coat, and the rumors are flying that he had a special radio receiver and he was getting answers from someone offstage. Wow, it's like he's back at Yale.

—David Letterman

For a long time, whenever the words *president* and *bulge* appeared in the same sentence, we were probably talking about Bill Clinton.

Hey, now!

But then came the great Bush-Bulge Caper of 2004.

The first debate between President Bush and John Kerry was held on September 30, 2004, in Miami, with Jim Lehrer acting as moderator. According to viewer polls and most nonpartisan analysts, the debate was pretty much a dead heat, with neither candidate delivering a "knockout punch" or making a memorable gaffe. (Almost nobody ever delivers a knockout punch in a debate, yet after every debate the pundits inevitably say, "There weren't any knockout punches." True, and there weren't any puppet shows either.)

However, there was something unusual about the evening, as first noted by blogger Joseph Cannon on the morning of October 2:

> While watching a re-broadcast of the debate, my ladyfriend noted something odd: Bush seemed to have a wire, or an odd protrusion of some sort, running down his back.
>
> Apparently, Fearless Leader used an earpiece.... This theory goes a long ways toward explaining the president's consistently odd speech patterns—the cavernous pauses punctuating sharp volleys of sound.

First off, you just gotta love anyone who refers to his "ladyfriend," all in one word like that. I would have thought that died with Sinatra or maybe LBJ, but there you have it. Also, I'm jealous of anyone who finds a ladyfriend who watches rebroadcasts of presidential debates.

Anyway, Cannon goes on to speculate that Bush might have been wearing a tiny "tooth-phone" or "molar mobile," that is, a wireless receiver that's actually embedded in a back molar and transmits sound waves painlessly from the tooth to the inner ear. (Note: There really is such a device.)

"How can we acquire proof?" wrote Cannon. "Simple. Someone close to the scene of the next debate has to find out the frequency Bush is using. Once again, a simple tape recorder can bring down a president."

Just like with Andrew Johnson! I mean Nixon.

A few days later, as speculation about the "Bush bulge" was running rampant on blogs and in chat rooms, Salon.com's Dave Lindorff picked up the ball with an article titled "Bush's Mystery Bulge."

"Bloggers are burning up their keyboards with speculation," wrote Lindorff.

> Check out the president's peculiar behavior during the debate, they say. On several occasions, the president simply stopped speaking for an uncomfortably long time and stared ahead with an odd

expression on his face. Was he listening to someone helping him with a response to a question? Even weirder was the president's strange outburst. In a peeved rejoinder to Kerry, he said, "As the politics change, the positions change. And that's not how a commander in chief acts. I, I, uh—let me finish—the intelligence I looked at was the same intelligence my opponent looked at."

The *Salon* piece quotes the owner of a high-tech surveillance shop, who says, "There's certainly something on [Bush's] back, and it appears to be electronic." The bulge "could be the inductor portion of a two-way push-to-talk system," wrote Lindorff.

A number of articles about the mysterious bulge made mention of an incident that summer at a D-Day memorial in France, when a CNN broadcast reportedly picked up a "mystery voice" saying a line just before Bush said the same line. Coupled with the photos of the strange bulge under Bush's suit jacket at the debate, there was your "proof" that the president of the United States was receiving on-the-spot coaching from some unseen advisor such as Karl Rove.

The story spread to the mainstream media, forcing the White House to issue some kind of a response.

"I think you've been spending a little too much time on conspiracy Web sites," Bush spokesman Scott Stenzel said when he was asked about the bulge during a *Washington Post* chat session. Stenzel also joked with reporters that "Elvis" would be moderating a future debate.

"It was most likely a rumpling of that portion of his suit jacket, or a wrinkle in the fabric," another spokesperson told the *New York Times.*

Yet another spokesman for the Bush campaign said the president had never used any kind of electronic communication device, either for coaching purposes or to alert him to a security situation. The Bush campaign also denied that the president was wearing a bulletproof vest, as some had speculated.

As the conspiracy theorists posted photos supposedly showing Bush wearing earpieces, the late-night talk show hosts peppered their monologues with jokes about the controversy.

"I thought George Bush looked great," said David Letterman. "He was wearing his three-piece bulge. . . . They have a picture of George Bush from the first debate and on his back there's this big, lumpy bulge. People were saying that's a radio receiver and someone is feeding him answers to questions. It turned out tonight, the first thing George W. did was show everyone that the bump in his jacket was just a flask."

Ouch.

Bush's tailor became the "get" interview of the week. He told the press the mysterious bulge was just a puckering of a seam when the president leaned forward and crossed his arms in a certain manner. (And if you've ever experienced a puckering of the seam, you know how uncomfortable that can be.)

The conspiracy theorists weren't convinced.

"Two points about that 'Now let me finish,'" wrote Joseph Cannon, the man whose "ladyfriend" first spotted the bulge:

> 1. [Bush] seems genuinely irritated, as though someone had just interrupted him. 2. In fact, no-one *had* interrupted him.
>
> Was he addressing Jim Lehrer? No, because the odd interjection came long before the flashing lights warned that his 90 seconds were up. . . . Bush's expression of irritation appears to have been directed at someone speaking to him, someone unheard by anyone else in the room.

It's so wacky you want to believe it's true—the idea that someone was feeding Bush his talking points and that for a moment Bush forgot about the subterfuge and blurted out "Let me finish!" like some character in a *Naked Gun* movie.

What's more likely is that Bush was responding to the green flashing light indicating he had about 30 seconds left. He got a little flustered, thought his time was about to run out, and said "Let me finish!"

As for the odd pauses, the vacant stares, the apparent lack of focus at times—since when has Dubya *not* acted and sounded that way in public?

Humor books are filled with "Bush-isms." The Internet is bulging (so to speak) with clips of Bush making verbal stumbles at one event after another. He is arguably the least articulate ad-libber of any president since, let's see, George Washington. If the same odd bulge had shown up in Bill Clinton's jacket, we would have thought it was a bulletproof jacket or perhaps some sort of sexual massage device. Nobody would have suggested that Clinton was wearing a two-way communications device, because he didn't need anybody's help in a debate situation.

George Bush? He needs help counting to 10, or so the easy jokes go. So it was easy to jump to the conclusion that he was wired for communication, like a quarterback getting the plays from the sidelines.

One thing, though: if the president had been using this high-tech version of a walkie-talkie for so long, why did he deliver such an average performance in that 2004 debate? I mean, if that's how he sounds when he's getting coached, is he completely incoherent on his own?

If the debate marked the first time Bush had ever used the device, that would mean he and his campaign team weren't just unethical; they were crazy. Wouldn't you want to "test-drive" such a tricky mechanism in less stressful conditions—say, a photo opportunity with some schoolchildren or something? ("Wow, the president seems to know all the words to "The Pet Goat" without even looking at the pages!")

It also seems like an incredibly risky proposition. The president of the United States, favored to win reelection, is going to risk his hold on the office by agreeing to get wired like that? Bush and his campaign team are going to open themselves up to international embarrassment and scandal and a lifetime of ridicule, knowing that all it would take is for one person to leak the story of the decade to the media?

Let's walk through the particulars for a moment. Say Karl Rove was ensconced somewhere in the building where the Miami debate took place. I suppose the Secret Service could sequester a room without explanation and the Bush team could set up some kind of command center with a TV monitor. And I suppose Rove could sit there with a few associates while the Secret Service stood guard outside, making sure no one could enter.

In the meantime, another team is prepping Bush for the debate—strapping the device around his torso, inserting the earpiece, making sure the whole thing is working. *Testing one two three, testing one two three, please remember that it's "nuclear" and not "nukular," Mr. President . . .*

Now the president is onstage, while Rove is in the secret room. Here comes the first question from the panel. Rove has to process the question, formulate an answer, and immediately start feeding those talking points to Bush, a la Albert Brooks's briefing of Holly Hunter, who in turns spoon-feeds information to William Hurt at the anchor desk in *Broadcast News.*

Bush has to regurgitate Rove's notes even as Rove is giving him the next talking point. That's a lot tougher than it sounds.

Even if all that really happened, why would Bush say "Let me finish" to his coach? If he's in the middle of giving an answer, he's not going to tell the unseen advisor to stop talking, since he needs the rest of the information *to* finish. (Unless Rove was criticizing Bush's answer, and Bush was getting ticked off with his adviser.)

Ah, but maybe Rove (or whoever) was just giving Bush a few talking points here and there. But if that's all it was, why bother with such an elaborate scheme?

I'd also like to think the White House would have a more sophisticated way of furnishing information to the president than some device you can buy on the Internet. At the very least, they'd custom-make a few suits so the bulge wouldn't be so obvious.

Unless, of course, the bulge was just the fabric bunching up.

26

BARACK OBAMA: RADICAL MUSLIM!

Though he's written two books about himself already, most people know very little about Barack Hussein Obama Jr.'s uncommonly privileged private life.

—From a typically "Fair and Balanced" Fox News report by Carl Cameron on *Special Report with Brit Hume*, December 5, 2006

The conspiracy to install a radical Muslim in the White House runs wide and deep, dating back nearly four decades and incorporating a wide range of nefarious characters, from former Black Panther Bobby Rush to the hot chick who played the character Seven of Nine on *Star Trek: Voyager*.

Uh-huh.

Hang with me on this one. Barack Obama became the instant "rock star" (to quote the overused cliche) of American politics when he gave the keynote address at the 2004 Democratic National Convention in Boston. Though he was just a state senator who had never held national office and was unknown to most of the country, the handsome and magnetic Obama delivered a passionate speech that instantly catapulted him into the ranks of serious contenders for the 2008 presidential nomination.

Funny thing is, Obama had once been considered a long shot to win the Senate race in Illinois. If someone had mentioned him as a presidential candidate a year earlier, even Obama would have laughed.

In 1996, Obama won election to the Illinois State Senate. In 2000 he tried to unseat four-term congressman Bobby Rush, but Rush toppled the little-known Obama by more than a two-to-one margin.

Of course, that was all part of the plan. Obama couldn't become a congressman because "they" had bigger things in store for him—like the United States Senate, and then the presidency!

In early 2004, though, Obama was just one contender in a crowded field of contenders for the Democratic nomination for the U.S. Senate. A *Chicago Tribune*/WGN-TV poll in February of that year found investment banker Blair Hull in the lead among Democratic candidates with 24 percent, followed by Obama with 15 percent, state comptroller Dan Hynes with 11 percent, and Cook County treasurer Maria Pappas with 9 percent.

Given that Hull planned to spend at least $40 million of his own money on his campaign, and Pappas and Hynes were Chicago political veterans with higher name recognition, Obama was facing an uphill struggle. I remember meeting an Obama campaign operative in a Chicago restaurant, and he was lamenting the reality that his candidate was such an unknown commodity. "If only people knew about my guy, he could be the next John Kennedy," said the operative.

It seemed as if Obama was destined to finish second at best. But then came the revelations that Hull had been involved in a nasty split-up with his third wife, who had also been his second wife, as they had divorced and then remarried. She had obtained orders of protection against him on two occasions, and according to a 1998 police report, he was accused of striking her on the shin.

Hull remained in the race, but his candidacy was dead. Obama left Pappas and Hynes in the dust and easily won the primary—but he still faced a formidable opponent in Republican candidate Jack Ryan, something of a golden boy himself.

With a name straight out of a Tom Clancy novel and a Kennedyesque head of hair, the Harvard-bred Ryan was a millionaire investment banker who retired from the business world to teach at an inner-city Chicago parochial school. He married actress Jeri Ryan, best known for her portrayal of the aforementioned Seven of Nine on *Star Trek: Voyager*, and they had a son. If you were casting a movie about a senator and his wife, you wouldn't cast the Ryans because they'd be *too* attractive.

But by the time Ryan was actually running for Senate, he was divorced—and it was the decision by a California judge in summer 2004 to release those divorce papers that led to Ryan's political demise.

In the files, Jeri Ryan alleged that during the marriage, her husband had taken her to sex clubs in New York, Paris, and New Orleans and had asked her to have sex with him while other couples watched.

Ryan said the allegations were overblown: "We did go to one avant-garde nightclub in Paris, which was more than either of us felt comfortable with. We left and vowed never to return."

Didn't matter. Like Hull, Ryan was a dead man running (for office). He dropped out of the race, blaming the media, and was succeeded by Alan Keyes, an out-of-state extremist who had a better chance of becoming the next "American Idol" than the next senator from Illinois.

Obama won the election in a landslide, thanks to a couple of very "convenient" scandals. Even before he was sworn in, people were talking about him as a presidential candidate.

Enter the Muslim element.

On December 18, 2006, far-right-wing hysteric Debbie Schlussel wrote a very subtle and understated column on her blog titled "Barack Hussein Obama: Once a Muslim, Always a Muslim."

Yes, and once an idiot, always an idiot.

Citing Obama's middle name, noting that his father was "apparently a Muslim," ominously adding that Obama's mother's second husband was Indonesian ("likely another Muslim, as Indonesia is

Muslim-dominated and has the largest Islamic population in the world"), and mentioning Obama's "born-again affinity" for his father's country of Kenya, Schlussel saw a very disturbing pattern.

"Is a man who Muslims think is a Muslim, who feels some sort of psychological need to prove himself to his absent Muslim father, and is now moving in the direction of his father's heritage, a man we want as president when we are fighting the war of our lives against Islam?" wrote Schlussel. "Where will his loyalties be?"

Schlussel was on to him! She had figured out that once Obama was in the White House, he'd strap on the turban and declare his loyalties to Osama bin Laden. She's brilliant, I tell you, brilliant!

More shit from Schlussel:

Is that even a man we'd want to be a heartbeat away from the presidency, if Hillary Clinton offers him the vice-presidential candidacy (which he certainly wouldn't turn down)?
NO WAY, JOSE.... Or, is that HUSSEIN?

The caps are hers, by the way. You can't invent people like this. Or clone them. Thank God.

Most rational people on all sides of the political debate recognize Schlussel as a fringe wannabe—a predictable nutball who would have to get a better dye job and dress sluttier to socialize at the same hateful cocktail parties as the likes of Ann Coulter. But the Obama/Muslim story picked up momentum with a "report" in *Insight* magazine—which is published by the ultraconservative *Washington Times*—that was picked up by (surprise!) the Fox News Channel and other hardcore conservative voices, such as the humorless Mark Steyn, a syndicated columnist who's just to the right of Atilla the Hun.

The *Insight* article claimed Obama was a student at a radical Muslim school, known as a *madrassa*. Just as nefarious (and untrue) were the allegations that Hillary Clinton's campaign had uncovered this information as part of a background check on Obama.

From the lead of the *Insight* article:

Are the American people ready for an elected president who was educated in a Madrassa as a young boy and has not been forthcoming about his Muslim heritage?

This is the question Sen. Hillary Rodham Clinton's camp is asking about Sen. Barack Obama.

An investigation of Mr. Obama by political opponents within the Democratic party has discovered that Mr. Obama was raised as a Muslim by his stepfather in Indonesia.

The article cites an unnamed source that claims, "Obama's education became a life-long relationship with Islam as a faith and Muslims as a community. This has been a relationship that contains numerous question marks."

In January 2007, Mark Steyn took up the cry in an allegedly humorous column dripping with sarcasm and resentment.

Barack Obama announced last week that he was forming an exploratory committee to explore whether he can really be as fabulous as the media say he is. And happily the answer is: yes! He's young, gifted and black, and white, and Hawaiian, and Kansan, and charismatic, and Congregationalist and Muslim.... He was raised in an Indonesian madrassah by radical imams, which is more than John Edwards can say....

Some commentators say he's a blank slate. And how long is it since we've seen one of those?

I'll bet in those radical madrassahs they're still using blank slates.

Yes, and blank slates are more unpredictable than Steyn's right-wing diatribes.

An unsigned e-mail (what, you thought it would be signed?) began making the rounds:

Obama takes great care to conceal the fact that he is a radical Muslim.... Since it is politically expedient to be a Christian when

> you are seeking political office in the United States, Obama joined
> the Church of Christ to help purge the notion that he is still a Muslim, which, ideologically, he remains today.

Hey that's the same trick lifelong Cubs fan Hillary Clinton tried to pull when she donned that Yankees cap to cater to New York voters!

When some responsible news organizations, including CNN and the Associated Press, checked out the Obama/madrassa story, it wasn't hard to debunk it.

CNN's senior international correspondent, John Vause, journeyed to the Basuki school in Indonesia, which Barack attended from 1969 to 1971. Vause found a public school, open to people of all faiths, with the students dressed in uniforms and the teachers wearing Western clothing.

Obama told Chicago's WLS–Channel 7, "When I was six, I attended an Indonesian public school where a bunch of the kids were Muslim, because the country is 90 percent Muslim. The notion that somehow, at the age of six or seven, I was being trained for something other than math is ludicrous."

The facts:

Barack Obama's biological father was born in Kenya. The elder Obama was brought up as a Muslim—not a radical Muslim, just a Muslim—and was agnostic by the time he married. Obama's parents divorced when Barack was just two. When Barack was six, his mother married an Indonesian man and they moved to Jakarta. He was there for four years, spending two years in the nonradical Muslim school and two years in a Catholic school.

Obama is a Christian. He is a member of the United Church of Christ. The school he attended for two years as a boy does not teach and has never taught radical Muslim beliefs.

Yet even after the story was refuted, some conservatives in the media wouldn't let it go. On John Gibson's radio show, he said that CNN's Vause "probably went to the very [same] madrassa" as Obama.

The conspiracy continues!

27

THE HATE CRIMES PREVENTION ACT

We would hope that Christians wouldn't commit acts of violence, but we know they do at times. Just because their victim is a homosexual, it doesn't mean they attacked the person for that reason.

—Barrett Duke, in an essay opposing hate crimes legislation on the Web site of the Ethics & Religious Liberty Commission of the Southern Baptist Convention

The bigoted and the intolerant love to rattle the Free Speech saber whenever they feel their rights to be ignorant are under siege. That's why the American Family Association sent out an "Action Alert" in summer 2007—they were worried that a bill presented to Congress would make it a "hate crime" for anyone, including priests and pastors, to speak out against homosexuality in any fashion.

From the Action Alert:

> Be one of one million Americans willing to take a stand in defense of two of our most precious freedoms—freedom of speech and freedom of religion. Here's why:

> A bill now before Congress would criminalize negative comments concerning homosexuality, such as calling the practice of homosexuality a sin from the pulpit, a "hate crime" punishable by a hefty fine and time in prison. This dangerous legislation would take away our freedom of speech and freedom of religion.

The Action Alert also contained misleading and erroneous categorizations of a California lawsuit, as well as the reasons why Gen. Peter Pace would be relinquishing his post as Joint Chiefs of Staff. (Despite the claims of the Action Alert, the California lawsuit was not about outlawing the use of words such as *marriage* and *union of a man and woman* in the workplace, and Pace did not step down because of his publicly expressed moral opposition to homosexuality.)

As for the Local Law Enforcement Hate Crimes Prevention Act of 2007—there was nothing in the bill making it illegal to make negative comments about homosexuality. Nor was there anything in the bill targeting speech from the pulpit. It was about crimes involving people who cause injury to another person based on gender, sexual orientation, or sexual identity. The bill even included specific language saying there was no intent to infringe upon First Amendment rights.

Nevertheless, Barrett Duke of the Ethics & Religious Liberty Commission wrote:

> Hate crimes legislation for homosexuals could also open the door to the prosecution of speech as a hate crime.... Hate crime legislation could be used to make speech against homosexuality a prosecutable offense, for example. Those who are offended by such speech could simply claim that they felt attacked by the "offensive" language.

Well, no.

And yet the Action Alert from the American Family Association urged followers to sign a petition that read, "To members of Congress: I strongly urge you to vote against the 'hate crimes' bill.

. . . I will not step aside and let a small group of homosexual activists take away my freedom of speech and freedom of religion."

How about stepping aside and letting someone read the friggin' bill to you so you understand nobody's trying to take away your right to make a fool of yourself?

You'd think one person at the AFA would have read the bill before embarking on such a wrongheaded campaign. Either that or they did read it and then deliberately mischaracterized it.

But that wouldn't be very Christian, would it?

IX

MOVIES

28

OF *SOYLENT GREEN* AND *MEN IN BLACK*: THE BEST AND WORST CONSPIRACY MOVIES EVER MADE

What's the thing people remember about the Gulf War? A bomb falling down the chimney. Let me tell you something: I was in the building where we filmed that with a 10-inch model made out of Legos.

—Robert De Niro as Conrad "Connie" Brean in *Wag the Dog*

Nobody loves a good conspiracy more than Hollywood screenwriters. Literally dozens of mainstream films must have started with a writer thinking of his favorite conspiracy theory and wondering, "What if it were *true*?"

That's almost always how it plays out. In the world of the movies, the conspiracy theory more often than not turns out to be a hell of a lot more than a theory. (After all, you wouldn't have much of a movie if Truman were wrong about things being kind of peculiar in *The Truman Show*.) Moviemakers love to tap into the conspiracy theorist in all of us, confirming our most creative fantasies and our deepest fears about the way things really work.

In the world of the movies, the government really does keep aliens preserved in tanks in underground labs, and men in black actually do hover above our cities in silent helicopters, and the news is indeed manipulated by the powers that be, and Lee Harvey Oswald truly was a patsy—sacrificed as part of a wide-ranging conspiracy to murder JFK.

From *The Firm* to *Conspiracy Theory* to *The Truman Show*, from *Three Days of the Condor* to *Outbreak* to *Mercury Rising*, from *Marathon Man* to *Shooter* to *The Da Vinci Code*, the hero is always convinced things are not what they seem to be, and everyone around him thinks he's crazy—but you know what? He's almost always right. There *is* a giant conspiracy at play, and it's up to our guy to expose it!

We love conspiracy movies because they usually give us that "Ah-ha!" moment that real life rarely provides.

When Kevin Costner delivers his entertaining but wildly implausible "magic bullet" speech in *JFK*, regurgitating the flawed-logic arguments we've heard for decades, the JFK assassination buffs say, "Ah-ha!"

When Richard Dreyfus comes over the hill and sees the spaceship welcome center in *Close Encounters of the Third Kind*, everyone who believes there's life among the stars says, "Ah-ha!"

When a trio of astronauts who are supposed to be flying to Mars are taken to a U.S. Army base and told they're going to have to fake the whole thing in *Capricorn One*, the diehards who are convinced we never made it to the moon say, "Ah-ha!"

If you held a Conspiracy Theorists Film Festival, you could start showing movies around the clock on Friday afternoon—and you'd just be getting warmed up by Sunday night.

◎

There's no set and single way to define a film as a conspiracy movie. Of course *The Manchurian Candidate* and *Wag the Dog* and *Men in Black* are conspiracy movies—but what about a legal thriller such as *The Firm* or an elaborate jigsaw puzzle con job such as *The Game*?

Those films aren't about elaborate, government-controlled conspiracies designed to keep the public in the dark concerning some great secret, but they are about sophisticated networks of individuals engaged in deceptive shadow operations. On its own level, *The Truman Show* is as much of a conspiracy movie as, well, *Conspiracy Theory*.

You could fill an entire book with a roster of conspiracy movies. For this section, we're going to concentrate on a selected sampling of films that have been released during my moviegoing lifetime. (Which means you can hold off on those e-mails asking me if I'm part of a conspiracy to keep the original *Manchurian Candidate* off this list.)

In no particular order, these are some of the best and worst conspiracy movies I've seen in the last 30-plus years.

THE BEST

Three Days of the Condor (1975): Robert Redford was in the midst of a golden career run in the late 1960s and early 1970s, and he delivered one of his best performances in this post-Watergate cat-and-mouse thriller that was all too perfectly suited for the heightened sense of cynicism and paranoia permeating the country. I can remember the trailer from the time, with Redford's Turner saying, "I'm just a reader!" as he tries to understand why his own government wants him dead.

Turner works for the CIA, but he's really just a reader, literally—a guy who sits with a few colleagues in a brownstone on Manhattan's Upper East Side, working his way through novels and short stories in search of clues and codes. It has to be the most uneventful job in the agency.

One day Turner goes out to lunch—and when he returns, he finds everyone in the office has been murdered.

As Turner discovers there's a CIA-within-the-CIA, he turns to Faye Dunaway for help (and for some hot sex). Director Sydney Pollack does a superb job of putting us in Turner's shoes as he learns his government will murder its own people if it means protecting the Middle Eastern oil interests. The outstanding cast includes Cliff Robertson, Max Von Sydow, and John Houseman. Even if the computer technology seems comically outdated, *Three Days of the Condor* retains its effectiveness as a twisting, turning, double-crossing thriller about one decent guy who stumbles into the most labyrinthine depths of the CIA's Department of Conspiracies.

The Game (1997): David Fincher's insanely unbelievable and relentlessly entertaining *The Game* is not a film that immediately comes to mind when one talks about the great conspiracy movies. It doesn't involve a military-industrial cone of silence, or a rogue warrior trying to prove there's a secret plot to control the world, or a seemingly crazy loner whose paranoid theories turn out to be spot-on.

But it is a conspiracy movie, and one that's great fun to watch—especially the first time around, when you have no idea what's coming, and then you think you have the answer, but then there's one more twist after that. And then one more. Sure, when you look back on the whole thing, you realize there's no way the adventure could have reached its final destination without falling apart, but so what? It's not how you dissect it; it's how you play *The Game*.

Michael Douglas is in his comfort zone playing Nicholas Van Orten, an obscenely wealthy and accomplished man who is given a unique gift on his 48th birthday, courtesy of his younger brother (played by Sean Penn). It's an elaborate game of real-world survival, and once Nicholas agrees to participate, he surrenders control of his life. He loses access to his money, his power, his identity—and at some point he comes to believe that the game is no game at all and that his life is in peril. Deborah Kara Unger is the dangerous, smoky blonde who reluctantly comes to believe his story, but then it appears she's part of the conspiracy, but maybe she's not, but then again maybe she is, and where does it all end? On a rooftop, with the wrong person dying.

We think.

Wag the Dog (1998): Can you imagine a nation engaging in a war with a second-tier opponent under false pretenses, just to distract the populace from the real crises facing a presidency?

Why it's absurd!

Nevertheless, that was the wacky premise of *Wag the Dog*, the wickedly funny satire with a biting script from Hilary Henkin and David Mamet, fast-paced and assured direction from Barry Levinson, and a top-level cast having great fun with the material.

Wag the Dog begins with a Clintonesque president accused of manhandling a teenage girl just weeks before the election. Robert De Niro's Connie Brean is a political consultant who comes up with a monumental distraction: they'll just invent a war against Albanian fundamentalist extremists, complete with a genuine All-American hero, and that'll divert attention from the whole groping-the-Firefly-girl thing.

Wag the Dog does a superb job of playing into our most cynical opinions of how politicians manipulate the media and how the media manipulate us. The nation sees a little Albanian girl (Kirsten Dunst!) narrowly escaping terrorists while cradling her kitten. We see an American actress playing the Albanian girl on a soundstage, cradling a bag of snack chips that will be digitally manipulated to turn into a kitten.

Orchestrating it all is Dustin Hoffman's Stanley Motss, a veteran Hollywood producer clearly modeled after Robert Evans. ("This is nothing. You think this is hard? Try a 10 A.M. pitch meeting, coked to the gills, and you haven't read the treatment. That's hard. This is easy.") It's Motss's idea to invent "Old Shoe," the soldier who escapes near-certain death in Albania and is brought back for a hero's welcome.

Of course, this is all just paranoid fantasy. Our government spin machine doesn't recruit prisoners to portray war heroes, a la *Wag the Dog*. It just takes the stories of real soldiers such as Jessica Lynch and Pat Tillman, and lets us believe the most heroic scenarios possible—until the messy truth surfaces.

Conspiracy Theory (1997): Made during a time when we could buy into the idea of Mel Gibson playing a crazed obsessive without calling it typecasting. This movie is pure soft-core porn for the conspiracy theorist, or at least a wish-fulfillment fantasy, in that the obligatory one person who comes to believe in the crackpot conspiracy "nut" is none other than Julia Roberts. Sweet!

Oh sure, Julia's Justice Department lawyer is initially frightened for her life when Gibson's Jerry stalks her like John Hinckley in his Jodie Foster phase—but there's always a flicker of belief and sympathy in her gorgeous eyes, a flicker that turns into a roaring flame when she realizes he's not just another crazy cabbie with multiple copies of *The Catcher in the Rye*, a locked pantry, and aluminum firewall covering the walls of his apartment.

Gibson is hilarious, scary, weird, and sympathetic as the wide-eyed Jerry Fletcher, a talk radio–loving cab driver who believes that certain dead celebrities aren't really dead, that there's no such thing as a random "accident," and that nothing is what it seems to be. When Jerry says, "The Vietnam War was fought over a bet Howard Hughes lost to Aristotle Onassis," he does so with complete confidence.

Jerry publishes a conspiracy theory newsletter with a grand total of five subscribers—but when some of the fried wires in his brain begin to reconnect and he starts edging closer to the truth, he's seen as a real threat. Black helicopters materialize above Manhattan, and Patrick Stewart appears as the embodiment of the let's-keep-this-to-ourselves government bad guy.

In *Conspiracy Theory*, a U.S. intelligence agent compares the government to a big family and says, "We're the uncle no one ever talks about." For the conspiracy theorist who never *stops* talking about the uncle no one ever talks about, this is juicy stuff.

Total Recall (1990): Like Mel Gibson's Jerry, Arnold Schwarzenegger's Doug Quaid is suffering from memory loss, but for Quaid, a happily married construction worker in the year 2084, the memory erasure is virtually 100 percent—while he's awake, that is. But Quaid keeps having these dreams about working as an intelligence agent on a colony in Mars.

Perhaps a visit to the mind-tripping Rekall Inc. will clear things up. Then again, something could go wrong and it might trigger a series of events that will blow his mind.

Based on the legendary Philip K. Dick's *We Can Remember It for You Wholesale*, this 1990 film directed by Paul Verhoeven was one of the most expensive movies ever made at the time, and it featured special effects that dazzled. (Now we see more impressive stuff on sci-fi series on basic cable.) When Doug takes a two-week "vacation of the mind," which is supposed to give him a simulated trip to Mars, he instead finds himself actually on Mars, living his real life and finding out that the quiet Earth-bound existence was all just a fantasy.

Or is it the other way around?

Quaid comes to believe his true purpose is to lead the resistance on Mars against the ruthless dictator played by Ronny Cox. (One character mocks Quaid for believing he's the victim of "an interplanetary conspiracy.") Rekall representatives try to convince him he's still on a mind-tripping vacation, his Mars girlfriend tries to convince him this is his real life, Sharon Stone wants him dead—and even when we think we've got it figured out, we're not entirely sure if Doug has succeeded in "un-erasing" his real memories or if the trip to Mars was only in his head.

Dark City (1998): This is one of the greatest and most underappreciated conspiracy movies of the last half-century. It's a beautifully shot, futuristic mind-game with some of the most haunting scenes and images of any movie I've ever seen—a sci-fi film noir that asks pointed questions about the very essence of human nature. If you can't remember anything about yesterday, does that make you a different person today? Alex Proyas's masterpiece is like *Metropolis* as reimagined by Rod Serling for an elaborate episode of *The Twilight Zone*.

Rufus Sewell stars as John Murdoch, who is part of a grand experiment conducted by alien beings known only as "the Strangers." They have collected literally hundreds of human beings and placed them in an elaborate but artificial "city" in which there is no daylight and all movement stops at the stroke of midnight—and when everyone wakes up again, their memories and personal histories have been altered.

The Strangers are conducting these experiments to gain insight into the inner workings of the human soul—but the humans aren't aware of this. These people, for the most part, believe they are who they are and they do what they do. They don't realize their programmed memories are telling them what to do and think.

Dark City doesn't manipulate our experience. It tells us early on that there really is an alien-induced conspiracy, and then it shows us the mighty, noble, heartbreaking struggle of one man trying to break free from the chains of that conspiracy.

Outbreak (1995): The most memorable scene in *Outbreak* involves a sneeze in a movie theater. We literally follow the sputum from that sneeze as it rains on other moviegoers' popcorn, who of course have no idea they're about to ingest a deadly virus that will turn their internal organs to useless goo. It's a gross and terrifying scene, preying on our darkest mid-1990s fears about infectious diseases that take root in the jungles of Africa and find their way to the States, killing everything and everyone. (Not that we still aren't worried about flesh-eating microbes and the like; it's just that other types of terror have moved to the forefront of our collective consciousness.)

With books like *The Hot Zone* topping the bestseller lists, Wolfgang Petersen's crackling and outlandish thriller arrived in theaters in spring 1995. We start with a flashback scene set in the 1960s, when an American military team carpet bombs an entire jungle camp that's been riddled with a deadly new virus—the "Motaba" bug. Thirty years later, Dustin Hoffman's Col. Sam Daniels, a medical researcher, discovers a strain of the Motaba virus in another African village. He warns his superiors—but of course they ignore those warnings, and soon the Motaba is making its way to the United States via an illegally smuggled monkey. In a brilliant but stomach-churning sequence, we see how the virus can be spread through a variety of fashions, from the sneeze in the theater to a grownup sharing a cookie with a little kid.

As Col. Daniels tries to trace and stop the virus, he uncovers a vast military conspiracy spearheaded by none other than Donald Sutherland. Fortunately, he's got Rene Russo, Kevin Spacey, and Cuba Gooding Jr. on his side.

Outbreak is a conspiracy theorist's delight, since the plot here involves the military, the government, *and* the science and medicine fields.

They're all in on it!

Men in Black (1997): Most conspiracy movies are symphonies of serious ideas. *Men in Black* is a bubblegum novelty song that has big fun with the whole world of the conspiracy theorist. It is the most cheerfully upbeat paranoid-fantasy film of its time.

You think aliens walk among us? I mean, that's the only explanation for the way some people act and look, right? Well, *Men in Black* says you're right: of course aliens walk among us. They're everywhere, posing as convenience store clerks, pawnshop owners, even dogs and movie stars. In fact our planet is a place of friendly refuge—as long as the aliens don't cause trouble or reveal themselves. If that happens, the Men in Black are on the case. Tommy Lee Jones is a deadpan gem as world-weary MIB Agent K, and Will Smith is at his double-taking best as trainee Agent J, who cannot believe what he's seeing. Filled with hipster humor and entertainingly gross humor, *Men in Black* has a lot of fun with the whole alien-conspiracy universe, giving us a world where the *Weekly World News* is more reliable than the *New York Times* and government secret agents carry around magic silver devices that will zap all alien encounters from our collective memory.

How do we know such a device doesn't exist in real life? Because if it *did* exist and a Man in Black used it on you, you wouldn't remember that, now would you?

The Truman Show (1998): One of the great perks of my job as cohost of *Ebert & Roeper* is the actual viewing experience. I see about 250 movies a year, and about 90 percent of those movies are shown in a private screening room. There are no trailers, no trivia quizzes, no advertisements for soft drinks or credit cards. If the movie is scheduled to start at 10 A.M., it starts at 10 A.M. The first thing I see: the opening credits. I deliberately try to avoid reading plot summaries or advance feature articles about the movies, in order to experience them in the "purest" state possible.

That was the way you wanted to see *The Truman Show* in 1998—with little or no inkling of the plot and nothing cluttering your mind prior to the start of the story.

If you were lucky enough to experience Peter Weir's masterpiece in such a vacuum, you could fully appreciate the scope of the conspiracy encompassing the happy-go-lucky Truman Burbank (Jim Carrey), who thinks he's living an ordinary but uneventful life in idyllic Seahaven, Florida.

Of course, everyone, from the mailman to his best friend to his wife, is in on the most elaborate candid camera stunt ever conceived. Truman's entire life is a reality TV show, played out on the world's biggest soundstage. All his world's a stage, and all the people merely players.

The Matrix (1999): "What is the Matrix?" That was the tag line in the cryptic ads that appeared in early spring 1999, in the days and weeks leading up to the release of a buzzed-about sci-fi thriller starring Keanu Reeves and Laurence Fishburne.

Sure, the posters had a cool look and the trailers promised some groundbreaking special effects. But the hero of this movie was going to be Keanu Reeves? The guy who always said "Whoa!" in the movies and clomped about in unlaced gym shoes, always looking like he either just got high or was about to get high?

An interesting choice, to say the least. But it was just one of many genius moves by the Wachowski brothers, who must have realized that Reeves's deadpan style would serve him well in the role of the rebel leader Neo in what would turn out to be one of the most influential, entertaining, and mind-bending trilogies in conspiracy movie history.

Even though I've seen all three *Matrix* movies twice and discussed them endlessly, I'm still not entirely sure what the hell they're all about. But I do know these films served up some brilliant and original special effects, a boatload of big ideas, great moments of dry wit, and some of the most creative battle sequences ever conceived.

To fully give *The Matrix* its due as a conspiracy film, you have to forget about all the confusing existential psychobabble and the increasingly creative special effects. Go back to the beginning, to a man named Thomas Anderson, a drone for a software company in year 1999.

But at home, Anderson works as a hacker named Neo. One day his computer tells him, "WAKE UP NEO. THE MATRIX HAS YOU. FOLLOW THE WHITE RABBIT."

One pill makes you larger, and one pill makes you small. . . .

With the help of Fishburne's Morpheus and Carrie-Anne Moss's Trinity, Anderson comes to embrace his true identity as Neo, who's much more than a hacker—he just might be "the One," the messianic leader of the ultimate rebel movement. Thomas Anderson's world is a computer-created virtual reality built by machines to control the thoughts of all human beings, who are actually trapped in the Matrix.

Whoa.

THE WORST

National Treasure (2004): My favorite moment in the howler that is *National Treasure* comes when Nicolas Cage's historical detective Ben Gates brings the Declaration of Independence—that's right, *the* Declaration of Independence, not a copy—to his estranged father's home, convinced there's a treasure map hidden on the back of the document.

The invisible map will reveal itself—if only they had some lemon juice to squirt on the document. Ben's dad, played by Jon Voight, opens the refrigerator—and bingo, there's an entire bowl of lemons! You know, just in case his estranged, map-detective son shows up in the middle of the night with the Declaration of Independence and needs to reveal a secret treasure map.

Cage is such an Indiana Jones knockoff in *National Treasure* that they should have named his character Illinois Smith. He's a history buff who becomes convinced there's that secret map on the back of the Declaration of Independence—and he steals the document just before an evil Englishman can get to it. He also convinces a historical archivist played by Diane Kruger to help him decipher the map, thus giving us the opportunity to confirm that the woman who played Helen of Troy is indeed among the worst actresses of our times. She's more wooden than the Babe Ruth bat collection in the Hall of Fame.

According to *National Treasure*, the famous Knights Templar treasure was amassed in the 11th century and was handed down through the centuries to a group that eventually became the Freemasons, and you know of course that many of this nation's Founding Fathers were Freemasons, which explains how the treasure came to the United States of America in the 1700s, where it was eventually buried in a bad Nicolas Cage movie.

The Net (1995): When was the last time you heard anyone refer to the Internet as "the Net"? Probably around 1995, when this silly and dopey computer conspiracy thriller was released.

Sandra Bullock—whose fresh-faced, chirpy persona does not immediately scream "Computer genius!"—plays a whip-smart systems analyst named Angela who spends nearly every waking hour attached to her comically dated computer. She never has any dates, she seems to have no personal life, and she rarely even leaves her house. When she wants food, she uses the computer to order a pizza. (This was a big selling point for the Internet back in the mid-1990s: "You'll be able to order a pizza right off your computer!" Wow, that's great, because picking up a phone and punching in the numbers was so exhausting and complicated.) Uh-huh. I guess there must be a home gym and a personal stylist located in a back room, because this supposed nerd-loner-computer whiz looks fantastic.

Just before Angela goes on her first vacation in nearly half a decade, she gains possession of a disk that would reveal the existence of the Praetorians, a secret society of cyber-criminals. The Praetorians use their cyber-powers to erase Angela's identity, to the point where another woman takes over Angela's life. And because Angela is such a loser and her mother has Alzheimer's, there exists not one human being in the entire world who can confirm that Angela is in fact Angela.

Uh-huh.

The only thing missing from this howler is a scene where Bullock looks to the sky, shakes her fist, and says, "Damn you, Praetorians! Damn you all to hell!"

Bug (2007): God, I hated this movie. As a stage play, it might have been effective and chilling and thought provoking. As a film, it's grotesque and ugly and ridiculous.

Michael Shannon plays Peter, a mysterious, intense drifter who looks like he's been hitchhiking and serial-killing his way across the country—but Ashley Judd's Agnes lets him into the dingy hotel room where she lives. She winds up sleeping with him because she's lonely and broke and desperate—her husband is a violent ex-con played by Harry Connick Jr. (!), so a creepy drifter guy doesn't seem so bad by comparison.

Only thing is, he's either infected with a government-induced virus, or he's the leading conspiracy theorist of the 21st century.

Peter wakes up one night believing he's been bitten by a tiny bug in Agnes's bed. He begins to see bugs everywhere. He convinces Agnes the bugs have infested her motel room. Soon he's yanking out his own teeth and cutting up his skin, convinced that the government has implanted listening devices and "egg sacs" of bugs in him as part of its attempt to cover up what he knows about . . . something.

Near the end of the movie, the blood-covered Peter begins spouting an endless stream of conspiracy theories, and Agnes is so far gone she's right there with him, and some guy claiming to be

Peter's doctor shows up, and we hear the faint whirring of helicopter blades above the motel, so we're not sure if he's crazy or if there really is some kind of government plot here—but by that point we don't care. Ashley tries to save the movie by whipping off her clothes for her obligatory "Mr. Skin" moment (she's vying with Sharon Stone for most naked scenes by an actress in motion picture history), but it's too late. She could jump off the screen and kiss you and it wouldn't matter.

Bug gets under your skin in a way that few films can match. You exit the experience feeling as if you need a delousing.

The Stepford Wives (2004): The original *Stepford Wives* from 1975 is most notable for spawning a pop culture catchphrase to describe a certain type of subservient suburban housewife stereotype.

The movie itself is highly overrated. It's one of those films that are called classics only by people who have never seen them. Granted, there's something original and intriguing about the creepy, misogynist, feminist-backlash concept, which has a group of men conspiring to turn their wives into obedient robots, as some sort of 1950s wish-fulfillment fantasy trip. But if you ever watch the original version, you'll be surprised at how silly and stupid it all looks.

Still, the 1975 version is a masterpiece compared with the 2004 remake starring Nicole Kidman.

The updated version of *The Stepford Wives* plays like a satire of the original—but the first edition was so campy and dopey, there's not much to lampoon. This time around, the women are successful achievers whose careers overshadowed their husbands'—until the guys discover a way to turn the women into tiara-wearing, bake sale–giving, submissive sex partners.

The Stepford Wives also contains one of the most glaring inconsistencies I've ever seen in a major film. We're told that the men implant computer chips in the women, which turn them into docile creatures, and that men can control their wives via remote controls. But then there's a scene in the film in which Kidman discovers a look-alike robot designed to take her place. It's supposed to be the

most shocking moment in the film, but it makes no sense whatsoever. If the men have successfully conspired to turn their own wives
into robotic creatures, what's the robot look-alike for?

The movie never explains it. You'd think somebody would have
noticed this problem during the editing process, but maybe everyone fell asleep.

JFK (1991): Oliver Stone's controversial epic about the assassination of John F. Kennedy isn't easily dismissed trash like *The Stepford
Wives*—it's an entertaining, provocative, well-made piece of trash.
One can admire Stone's filmmaking skills and the performances
here while denouncing the utter crapola presented as "evidence" of
a conspiracy to murder Kennedy.

JFK is a more offensive film than the likes of *National Treasure*
and *The Net*, because it has ambitions far beyond a conspiracy theory adventure story. It's trying to be an important argument about
one of the key moments in American history—but it's actually less
plausible than Nicolas Cage running around with a rolled-up Declaration of Independence and trying to find the long-lost treasure
of the Knights Templar.

The casting of Kevin Costner, the Jimmy Stewart of American
cinema at the time, as New Orleans district attorney Jim Garrison,
lends instant credibility to the character of the conspiracy-obsessed
DA. When Costner commands the courtroom and delivers an
impassioned monologue about the so-called "magic bullet," it's
easy to laugh at the lone-gunman theory and buy into the seemingly logical argument presented by Garrison—that is, if you haven't
read the evidence and the materials that make the magic bullet nonsense disappear in a puff of wishful thinking.

Using a dazzling array of filmmaking techniques and a stellar
roster of actors including Sissy Spacek, Jack Lemmon, Kevin Bacon,
Tommy Lee Jones, Ed Asner, Joe Pesci, and Walter Matthau, Stone
bombards us with snippets of rumor, innuendo, and urban legend.
He argues that the photo of Oswald with a rifle that wound up on
the cover of *Life* magazine was a fabrication. He creates a Pentagon official known as "Mr. X," played by Donald Sutherland. He

wants us to believe the coconspirators included an American businessman named Clay Shaw, a former FBI agent, a mobster, some Cuban exiles, and just maybe Colonel Mustard with a candlestick. Mr. X explains it all in convoluted fashion to Garrison, who actually says, "I never realized Kennedy was so dangerous to the Establishment!"

As a work of fantastical fiction, *JFK* is an interesting if overblown vision of a parallel universe. As a dramatic interpretation of events, it's journalistically bankrupt nonsense.

The Island (2005): Here's one conspiracy I believe to be 100 percent true: in *The Island*, the filmmakers teamed up with companies ranging from Aquafina to Puma to Calvin Klein to Apple to create one of the most blatant product-placement movies of all time.

As for the actual conspiracy unfolding here: after a cataclysmic disaster on Earth, only a few hundred lucky survivors exist. Soon they'll be living on a paradise known as "the island," but for now they're contained in a gigantic indoor colony, where they can be kept safe from contamination.

At least that's the story implanted in the false memories of the inhabitants of the colony, including Ewan McGregor's Lincoln Six-Echo and Scarlett Johansson's Jordan Two-Delta, who have begun to develop feelings for each other despite strict rules against such fraternization.

The curious Lincoln Six-Echo has a hunch everything's not what it's supposed to be—and he discovers that he and Jordan Two-Delta and everyone else in the facility are actually clones, "born" fully grown and kept alive for organ harvesting. In the real world, there's a race car driver who looks just like the McGregor clone, and his liver's failing, and it's only a matter of time before Clone-boy is sliced and diced and discarded.

The Island rips off elements of films ranging from the howler *The Clonus Horror* to *Blade Runner*, *Coma*, and *Minority Report*. It's a $100 million B-movie with classy actors spouting ridiculous sci-fi dialogue while engaging in loud, expensive, blue-screen stunt sequences. In the hands of bombastic director Michael Bay, it's slick but cheesy, fast paced but illogical. Nearly everything and everyone eventually blows up, including the story.

Mercury Rising (1998): The conspiracy in *Mercury Rising* goes all the way to the highest levels of the government. It goes all the way to . . . Alec Baldwin!

Baldwin's portrayal of an evil colonel is about the only worthwhile element in this cloying conspiracy thriller. There are some other good actors here, including Chi McBride and Kim Dickens, but they don't stand a chance against the cliche-riddled screenplay.

Here's the deal. For years, the National Security Agency has been developing the most sophisticated code humankind has ever known.

So how does the NSA test the code? By placing it in a puzzle magazine.

Not that there's anything to worry about. The code is so sophisticated it can't be cracked by computer, let alone a human being.

Unless that kid happens to be little Simon, a nine-year-old autistic savant who calls the phone number embedded in the code, setting off a panic attack within the NSA. The kid's parents are assassinated, but he manages to hide from the bad guys until he's found by rogue cop Bruce Willis, who spends the rest of the movie protecting the kid and solving the mystery.

Willis was "awarded" the 1999 Golden Raspberry for Worst Performance by an Actor, but I'm sorry to say it was the little kid playing the autistic boy who delivered one of the worst performances by a child actor I've ever seen. Rolling his eyes into the back of his head, shrieking, and overacting—it's painful to watch. I'm not mentioning the kid's name here because it seems gratuitously mean, but according to the Internet Movie Database (www.imdb.com), he continues to act, with one of his more recent roles being "Stoner Dude #1" on an episode of *Veronica Mars.*

So he's got that going for him, which is nice.

Shooter (2007): You gotta love it when movie characters have names that describe the way they walk. In *Shooter*, Mark Wahlberg is Swagger. (No word on whether he has brothers named Saunter and Strut.) He's a highly trained military sniper who is left out to dry by his own company on a mission in Ethiopia that leaves his best friend dead.

Disillusioned and disgruntled, Swagger leaves the military and holes up in a mountain hideaway, where he spends his days hunting with his trusty dog and logging onto conspiracy Web sites.

One day Danny Glover's Col. Isaac Johnson shows up at Swagger's place and explains there's a plot afoot to assassinate the president of the United States. Perhaps Swagger could use his sharpshooting training and military expertise to demonstrate if the planned assassination is even possible? He could walk them through the paces from the assassin's point of view. It would be a great service to his country.

Now, you'd think a paranoid, disenfranchised former military man might smell a conspiracy afoot—but Swagger goes along with the plan, realizing far too late that his own government has set him up. Dude, they asked you to *impersonate an assassin*. What'd ya think that was all about?

Before you know it, Swagger's a wanted man and he's on the run, trying to prove his innocence and nail the conspirators, which include several top military brass and a corrupt senator, played by the red-faced Ned Beatty in all his hammy glory.

Shooter wants to be *Rambo* with a conspiracy twist. At one point Levon Helm, who used to be in a band called the Band, shows up to spout some classic conspiracy theories. It would be one thing if Helm's monologue were there for comic relief, but I think we're supposed to believe him. Lord help us.

The Wicker Man (2006): Hey, it's not my fault that Oscar-winner Nicolas Cage stars in two of the worst conspiracy movies in recent memory. He's the one who cashed a paycheck for *National Treasure*, and he's the one headlining the god-awful remake of *The Wicker Man*, which comes to its conclusion with Cage running around a remote island in a bear suit, trying to avoid human sacrifice at the hands of a gang of murderous man-hating women who want him killed as part of their annual Day of Death and Rebirth Celebration. For real.

Cage plays a California highway patrolman who receives a letter from a long-lost girlfriend telling him their daughter has gone missing on a small island in the Pacific Northwest. The women on this island dress like the characters in *The Village* and talk like they're Amish; they're led by Ellen Burstyn, who is called Sister Summersisle. She's kinda like Kathy Bates in *Misery* crossed with the nun who taught Jake and Elwood in *The Blues Brothers*.

The original cult classic version of *The Wicker Man*, released in 1973, featured lots of nudity. The remake features women in beekeeping garb and Cage in that bear suit, running around and punching out the gals who are trying to tie him up and burn him alive.

Apparently these women are all part of a conspiracy to torpedo Nicolas Cage's credibility.

The Star Chamber (1983): As any card-carrying conspiracy theorist can tell you, the world is run by a cabal of older white men in suits who gather in back rooms and decide everything, from the value of the dollar to the next war to the outcome of the NBA finals. In the well-made but exploitative film *The Star Chamber* (so titled as a reference to the powerful English court at Westminster Abbey from the late 1400s to the mid-1600s), the secret society legend is turned into a *Death Wish* fantasy.

Frustrated when killers are set free because of loopholes in the legal system, a group of judges meets behind closed doors and returns verdicts without such bothersome elements as defense attorneys and due process. And then they, in the words of Hal Holbrook, "do something about it."

In other words, they hire an assassin to kill the criminal.

Holbrook, the go-to guy for playing seemingly respectable authority figures with dark secrets, plays a judge who hosts the Star Chamber sessions in a tastefully appointed conference room in his home. No word on who decorated it. *The Star Chamber* could have been an interesting commentary on the justice system, but it devolves into a standard thriller that ends up with the obligatory shoot-out that makes no sense.

I believe there's a conspiracy afoot to have four out of every five thrillers ever made end with a shoot-out in an abandoned warehouse, usually by the docks.

AND THREE GUILTY PLEASURES

Granted, these three conspiracy movies are riddled with plot holes and some unintentionally funny moments, but they're a lot of fun and I can't resist 'em.

***Capricorn One* (1978):** When I saw the trailers for this film as a high schooler, I thought it looked like it just might be the coolest idea for a movie I'd ever seen. Then again, I thought *Capricorn One* star O. J. Simpson was pretty cool at the time, too. Things change.

Capricorn One, written and directed by Peter Hyams, who also directed *The Star Chamber*, has a tantalizing setup that must have had the moon-landing nonbelievers salivating. And look, there's Hal Holbrook, once again playing an authority figure with something nefarious up his sleeve.

Holbrook plays a NASA director overseeing the first manned flight to Mars. Knowing the mission has no chance of succeeding, Holbrook has the three astronauts (played by Sam Waterston, James Brolin, and O. J. Simpson) transported to a deserted U.S. Army base, where they are told they will be faking the Mars landing.

Of course! Only an idiot would believe humans could travel to the moon or another planet!

Before it's all over, the astronauts realize that for the conspiracy to work, they'll have to be eliminated. They try to escape, and that's when we cue the black helicopters.

Capricorn One doesn't exactly explain how a faked NASA launch could actually work, but the first half is great fun and the ending is satisfying albeit corny. The difference between most conspiracies and most conspiracy movies is that in the movies, the conspirators are *busted*.

Soylent Green (1973): WARNING: *There's no way to talk about the camp value of this film without giving away the ending. If you haven't seen* Soylent Green *and you want to check out an entertaining if somewhat campy conspiracy thriller with a twist, skip this entry for now.*

For every person who has actually seen the 1973 sci-fi conspiracy film *Soylent Green* there are probably 50 people who know the famous line from Charlton Heston: "Soylent Green is people!"

It was voted one of the 100 greatest lines by the American Film Institute, and it's been the basis for dozens of jokes, as well as a spoof on *Saturday Night Live*, with Phil Hartman doing a hilarious impersonation of Heston. You can't hear the line now without chuckling—but when I first saw *Soylent Green* on late-night TV as a kid and Charlton Heston bellowed that chilling revelation, it was pretty cool stuff.

Soylent Green is set in 2022—and like 99 percent of movies set in the future, things aren't looking good. Global warming and overpopulation have nearly destroyed the planet. The population of New York City is at 40 million and counting. Only the elite of the elite can afford food as we know it and a decent education; most citizens are illiterate and poor, reduced to waiting in endless lines for processed food from the powerful Soylent Corporation.

Chuck Heston plays the police detective who finally discovers the secret ingredients of Soylent Green. It must have been great fun for audiences in the 1970s when that twist ending was revealed. At this point I don't know if there's anyone left who doesn't know the secret—but even if you know how it turns out and you find yourself laughing at the cheesy sets and overwrought dialogue, *Soylent Green* has some intriguing ideas and features one of Heston's better performances. In the scene where Heston cries as his mentor played by Edward G. Robinson says good-bye, the tears are real—for in real life, Heston knew that his longtime friend was actually dying. This would be Robinson's last film.

The Forgotten (2004): Julianne Moore is so fragile and so intense and so lovely and so vulnerable onscreen that she can go through entire movies looking like she's about to burst into flames at any moment. Such is the case with her passionate and slightly loopy performance in *The Forgotten* as a mother whose nine-year-old son dies in a plane crash. At least that's what she thinks happens—until the photos of her son disappear from the family mantel, and the news stories about the plane crash are erased from the archives, and everyone (including her husband) tells her she never had a son—that he's a psychological creation of hers, invented after she suffered a late-term miscarriage.

Jules isn't buying it. She hooks up with a drunken ex-hockey player who lost a daughter but has been told that she's a figment of his imagination, and soon we're knee-deep into a conspiracy thriller that could have interplanetary implications.

After a near-perfect setup, *The Forgotten* careens into eyebrow-raising territory, with some pretty incredible special effects that unfortunately are a little reminiscent of the famous bridge scene in *Monty Python and the Holy Grail.* It's a tricky thing, plucking people off the ground and into the sky.

The *New York Times* called *The Forgotten* a "pseudospiritual, mumbo-jumbo, science-fiction inflected mess," to which I say, well, *yes*, but it's ludicrous fun.

INDEX

A

A-3 Skywarrior engine, 7

Abdul, Paula, 119, 122

Absolute Poker Web site scandal, 63–64

Adams, Cecil, 191

AFA. *See* American Family Association

Aiken, Clay, 119, 120, 140

Air Fones, 15–16

Akeelah and the Bee, 129

Alliance Defense Fund, 166

Amazing Race, The, 118

Ameche, Alan, 70–71

American Airlines Flight 77, 8

American Civil Liberties Union (ACLU), 173–174

American Family Association (AFA), 166–167

    Action Alert, 209–211

American Football League (AFL), 74

American Idol, 117–123

American Justice Federation, 19

Amoss, Jim, 52

Aniston, Jennifer, 140

Answer Bitch, 140

Anthony, Susan B., 188

Apostolate of a Silent Soul, Inc., 159

Arenas, Gilbert, 80

Arnot, Bob, 34–35

Asner, Ed, 229

Assassination of JFK Jr.—Murder by Manchurian Candidate, 32–33

Avery, Dylan, 6, 8

B

Bacon, Kevin, 229

"bad beat" (poker), 60

Baldwin, Alec, 231

Baltimore Colts, 67–72, 74–77

Barr, Douglas William, Sr., 87

Barrino, Fantasia, 119

Basinger, Kim, 92

Beck, Glenn, 55

Bettis, Jerome, 78

Beverage Marketing Corporation, 141

bin Laden, Osama, 7

bird flu, 135–138

Black, Lewis, 128

"Black Sox" scandal, 82

Blade Runner, 230

Boston Red Sox, 91–96

Botham, Noel, 25
bottled water craze, 140–141
boycotts
    dollar coin, 188–189
    French products/services, 180
    gasoline, 177–180
    Starbucks, 129–130, 131
Bozell, Brent, 56
Broadcast News, 202
Brolin, James, 234
Brooks, Albert, 202
Brown, Kwame, 80
Brown, Larry, 74
Browne, Sylvia, 147–148
Buchanan, Pat, 55
Buck, Joe, 79
Bug, 227–228
Bullock, Sandra, 226–227
Burlingame, Charles, 7
Burstyn, Ellen, 233
Bush, George W., 31, 168–169
    "bulge" mystery, 197–202
    JFK Jr. death and, 31, 33
    worldview of, 177
Byrd, James, Jr., 42
Byrne, Rhonda, 108, 111–112

C

Cabrera, Ryan, 140
Cage, Nicolas, 225–226, 232–233
Cameron, Carl, 203
Cannon, Joseph, 198, 200
Capricorn One, 216, 234–235
card counting, 86–87
Carlson, Tucker, 48
Carrey, Jim, 224
casinos
    cheating, 84–85
    culture, 83–90

games, percentages, 85
    moneymaking techniques, 88–90
Catholic League for Religious and
    Civil Rights, 166–167, 168–169
Challenger disaster, 193–194
Chapman, Stephen, 56
Charen, Mona, 56
Chase, David, 100, 101
    comments of, 103
Chase, Vincent, 181
Chavez, Linda, 55
Cheadle, Don, 62
Cheney, Dick, 33
Children of Men, 47
chip-dumping (poker), 63–64
Christian, Channon, 39–46
Christmas, "war" on, 165–175
Christmas in Heaven (Browne), 147
Clancy, Tom, 204–205
Clark, Corey, 122
Clark, Dick, 119
Clarkson, Kelly, 119
Clinton, Bill, 169, 184, 197, 201, 219
Clinton, Hillary, 22, 206–207, 208
Clinton Body Count, 19–22
*Clinton Chronicles: An Investigation
    into the Alleged Criminal Activ-
    ities of Bill Clinton*, 21
Clonus Horror, The, 230
*Close Encounters of the Third
    Kind*, 216
cold readings, 146–147
Coleman, Susan, 20, 21
Colmes, Alan, 48
Color Purple, The (Broadway produc-
    tion), 119
Colts, Baltimore, 67–72, 74–77
Coma, 230
Compass, Eddie, 48–49

Conspiracy Theory, 216, 220
Cooper, Gary, 91
Costner, Kevin, 216, 229
Coulter, Ann, 55, 166, 206
Cowell, Simon, 119
Crossing Over, 145
CSI: Crime Scene Investigation,
    102, 123

D

Dancing with the Stars, 123
Daniels, Charlie, 41
Dark City, 221–222
Daughtry, Chris, 119
Da Vinci Code, 103, 216
Davis, Sammy, Jr., 182
De Niro, Robert, 215, 219
DeGeneres, Ellen, 109
*Designing Casinos to Dominate the
    Competition* (Institute for the
    Study of Gambling), 87
Desperate Housewives, 118, 123
Diana, Princess, 23–27
Dick, Philip K., 221
dollar coins, 187–190
Donaghy, Tim, 82
Donahue, William, 168, 169
Douglas, Michael, 218
Dreyfus, Richard, 216
drink urban legends, 183–185
Drudge, Matt, 55
drug urban legends, 183–185
Duke, Barrett, 209
Duke University lacrosse team allega-
    tions, 43–45
Dunaway, Faye, 218
Dunkleman, Brian, 119
Dunphy, Jack, 43
Dunst, Kirsten, 219

Duyser, Diane, 156–157

E

Ebert, Roger, 107
Ebert & Roeper, 224
Edward, John, 145, 148
Eisenhower, Dwight D., 169
Elrich, Dwight, 171
"Ether Zone Staff," 20
Ethics & Religious Liberty Commis-
    sion, 210
Ethos bottled water, 128
Evian bottled water, 139–141
Ewbank, Weeb, 70–71
Excluded Persons List (Nevada Gam-
    ing Commission), 87
eyewitness accounts, inaccuracy of,
    6–7

F

Falwell, Jerry, 166
    lawsuit, threat, 169–170
    promotion of *Clinton Chroni-
    cles*, 21
Farah, Joseph, 169
Fayed, Dodi al, 25, 26–27
Fayed, Mohammed al, 23, 25–26
Fear Factor, 122
Fear Strikes Out, 91
Fincher, David, 218
Fineman, Howard, 79
Firm, The, 216, 217
Fishburne, Laurence, 224, 225
Flight 77 (American Airlines), 8
Flight 93 (United Airlines), 8, 15–16
Forgotten, The, 236
Foster, Vincent, 20, 21
Francona, Terry, 93
Frey, James, 107

"Frozen Envelope" theory, 80–81
fuel-efficient cars, 178–179

G

Gaddafi, Muammar, 24
Game, The, 217, 218–219
game-fixing rumors (NFL), 81–82
Gandolfini, James, 103
gasoline boycotts, 177–180
Giants, New York, 67–72, 73
Gibson, John, 166, 172–174, 208
Gibson, Mel, 215, 220
Glover, Danny, 232
Godfather, The, 102
Goldberg, Bernard, 55
Gooding, Cuba, Jr., 223
Gore, Al, 33
Gray, John, 106
Green, Seth, 181

H

Hannity, Sean, 55
Hardaway, Penny, 80
Harris, Misty, 184
Hartman, Phil, 235
Hasselbeck, Elisabeth, 10
hate crimes
    alleged cover-up of, 39–46
    legislation, 209–211
    terminology, 44
Haykal, Mohammad Hassanein, 24
Henkin, Hilary, 219
Heroes, 99
Heston, Charles, 235
Hitler, Adolph, 192
Hobbs, Roy, 91–92
Hoffman, Dustin, 219, 222
Holbrook, Hal, 233, 234
Holmgren, Mike, 77

Holy Virgin Grilled Cheese, 156–157
Hornbeck, Shawn, 147
Hornung, Paul, 82
hot readings, 146–147
Hot Zone, The (Preston), 222
How I Met Your Mother, 183
Hudson, Jennifer, 121
Hull, Blair, 204–205
Hunter, Holly, 202
Hurricane Katrina, 47–53
Hurt, William, 202
Hynes, Dan, 204

I

Idiocracy, 133
*In the Kitchen with Rosie: Oprah's
    Favorite Recipes* (Daley),
    105–106
insider trading (9/11), 15
Institute for the Study of Gambling
    and Commercial Gaming, 87
*Interference: How Organized Crime
    Influences Professional Football*
    (Moldea), 71
Internet poker, 59–65
Island, The, 230–231
Iverson, Allen, 167–168

J

Jackson, Jesse, 41
Jackson, Randy, 119
JAG, 100
Jager Bombs, 181–185
James, LeBron, 82
jet fuel, 4–5
Jets, New York, 73, 74–77
Jews
    9/11 conspiracy theory, 15
    and "war" on Christmas, 173

JFK, 216, 229–230
Johansson, Scarlett, 230
Johnson, Andrew, 198
Jones, Tommy Lee, 223, 229
Jordan, Michael, 80, 81, 182
junk food urban legends,
   183–185

K

Karras, Alex, 82
Kennedy, John F., Jr.
   alleged assassination of, 29–35
   Nostradamus prediction regard-
     ing, 193
Kerry, John, 197
Keyes, Alan, 205
Kidman, Nicole, 228
King, Larry, 109, 147

L

Law & Order, 150
left-wing conspiracy, 55–56
Lemmon, Jack, 229
Leotardo, Nikki, 101
Letterman, David, 197
Levinson, Barry, 91, 219
Limbaugh, Rush, 55
Lindorff, Dave, 198–199
Little Audrey Fact Sheet, 160
Livingston, Kari, 120–121
Local Law Enforcement Hate Crimes
   Prevention Act of 2007, 210
Long, Shelley, 119
Loose Change, 6–9
Lost, 118

M

Madonna, 140
madrassa, 206

Malakar, Sanjaya, 117–118, 122
Malkin, Michelle, 55
   on Newsom/Christian murders,
     42–43, 44
Mamet, David, 219
Manchurian Candidate, The, 30, 32, 217
Marathon Man, 216
Marshall, Neil, 192–193
Martha's Vineyard, 34
Matrix, The, 224–225
Matthau, Walter, 229
McCartney, Paul, 129
McDougal, Jim, 20–21
McGregor, Ewan, 230
McKibbin, Nikki, 118
McLaughlin, John, 55
McPhee, Katherine, 121
media
   alleged liberal bias of, 39, 46,
     55–56, 166–168, 205
   "cover-ups," 30–31, 39–46
   coverage of miracles, 154–155,
     156–157
   and Hurricane Katrina, 39–46
Memory Almost Full (McCartney), 129
Men in Black, 215, 217, 223
Mercury Rising, 216, 231
Metropolis, 221
Mientkiewicz, Doug, 95
Million Little Pieces, A (Frey), 107
Minority Report, 230
Mirabelli, Doug, 93–95
miracles, claims of, 153–161
Moldea, Dan, 71
Monty Python and the Holy Grail, 236
Moore, Julianne, 236
Moss, Carrie-Anne, 225
Murder of Princess Diana, The
   (Botham), 25

Murdoch, Rupert, 55
Myers, Richard, 33

N

Nagin, Ray, 49
Naidu, Ajay, 183
Namath, Joe, 67, 73, 74–77
National Football League (NFL), 67–82
National Treasure, 229, 225–226
Natural, The, 91, 93
Net, The, 229, 226–227
Nevada Gaming Commission and State Gaming Control Board, 87
Neville, Arthel, 48–49
New Conspiracy Reader, The (Tuohy), 72–73
New England Patriots, 73–73
New Orleans, 47–53
New York Giants, 67–72, 73
New York Jets, 73, 74–77
New York Yankees, 92–93, 95, 96, 208
Newman, Paul, 190
Newsom/Christian murders, 39–46
Nichols, Lisa, 110–111
9/11 attacks, 1–17
Nixon, Richard M., 198
Noonan, Peggy, 56
North, Oliver, 56
North Star Zone (conspiracy Web site), 30
Nostradamus, 191–194

O

O, the Oprah Magazine, 106
Obama, Barack, 203–208
O'Donnell, Neil, 74
O'Donnell, Rosie, 3, 9–13

Office, The, 183
online poker, 59–65
Oprah Winfrey Show, The, 49
O'Reilly, Bill, 55
    French boycott call by, 180
    and "war" on Christmas, 165–168, 170–172
O'Reilly Factor, The, 141
Otto, Doug, 172
Outbreak, 216, 222–223

P

Pace, Peter, 210
Paige, Woody, 95
Palmer, Jim, 93
Pappas, Maria, 204
Park, Chan Ho, 79
Parker Bowles, Camilla, 28
Patriots, New England, 73–73
Paul, Henri, 26
Penn, Sean, 218
Penn & Teller, 141, 148
Pentagon attack, 4, 5, 7–8, 14–16
Perkins, Tony, 91
Pesci, Joe, 229
"Pet Goat, The," 201
pet psychics, 151–152
Peyser, Andrea, 56
Philpin, John, 44
Pittsburgh Steelers, 77–79
poker, 59–65
PokerStars (online gambling), 59, 64
Poker Room (online gambling), 59–60
Pollack, Sydney, 218
Presley, Elvis, 182, 199
Pride of the Yankees, 91
Princess Diana, 23–27
Proctor, Bob, 108
Proyas, Alex, 221

psychics
  alleged communication with dead,
    145–151
  for pets, 151–152
Psychic's Tour of the Afterlife, The
    (Browne), 147

R

Raiser, C. Victor, 20, 21
Rambo, 232
Randi, James, 148
Red Hot Chili Peppers, 140
Red Sox, Boston, 91–96
Redford, Robert, 91, 190, 217
Rees-Jones, Trevor, 26
Reeves, Keanu, 224
religious visions, 153–161
Rense.com, 30
Ripken, Cal, Jr., 79
risk/reward factor, 64, 81, 84–85, 90
Roberts, Cokie, 55
Roberts, Julia, 220
Robinson, Edward G., 235
Rose, Pete, 79, 82
Rosenbloom, Carroll, 69–72, 75
Rove, Karl, 201–202
Rumsfeld, Donald, 33, 125–138
Rush, Bobby, 204
Russo, Rene, 223
Ryan, Jack, 204–205
Ryan, Jeri, 205

S

Sanjaya, 117–118, 122
Santa Claus, 173–174
Santo, Audrey Marie, 158–161
Savage, Michael, 55
Scarborough, Joe, 56
Schilling, Curt, 91–96

Schlussel, Debbie, 205–206
Schwarz, Karl, 7
Schwarzenegger, Arnold, 221
Scrubs, 183
Seacrest, Ryan, 119
Seattle Seahawks, 67, 77–79
Secret, The, 105–115
September 11 attacks, 1–17
Serling, Rod, 221
Sewell, Rufus, 222
Shannon, Michael, 227
Sharpton, Al, 41, 48
Shepard, Matthew, 42
Shooter, 216, 232
Shula, Don, 76
"Silent Night," 170–171
Silverstein, Larry, 10, 12
Simpson, Ashlee, 140
Simpson, O. J., 234
SkepticReport Web site, 148
Smith, Bubba, 76
Smith, Sam, 80
Smith, Will, 223
Sopranos, The, 99–103
Soylent Green, 215, 235
Spacek, Sissy, 229
Spacey, Kevin, 223
spatial disorientation, 34
Star Chamber, The, 233–234
Star Search, 118
Star Trek: Voyager, 205
Starbucks, 127–133
Steelers, Pittsburgh, 77–79
Stenzel, Scott, 199
Stepford Wives, The, 228–229
Stephens, Donald, 157
Stern, Howard, 118, 122
Stevenson, McLean, 119
Steyn, Mark, 206

Sting, The, 190
Stone, Bob, 34
Stone, Sharon, 228
Stossel, John, 141
Straight Dope, The (Adams), 191
Studdard, Ruben, 120
Super Bowl, 67–68, 72–79, 82
Sutherland, Donald, 223, 229

T

Tamiflu, 137
Ted Mack's Amateur Hour, 118
Think Progress Web site, 171
Thomas, Cal, 55
Thompson, Linda, 19
Thorne, Gary, 93, 95
Three Days of the Condor, 216, 217–218
tooth-phone, 198
Total Recall, 221
Truman Show, The, 215, 217, 224
Tuohy, Brian, 72–74
24, 228
Twilight Zone, 103, 221

U

Underwood, Carrie, 119
Unitas, Johnny, 70–71, 75
United Airlines Flight 93, 8, 15–16
Unlawful Internet Gambling Enforcement Act of 2006 (UIGEA), 59–60

V

Van Susteren, Greta, 48, 50
Vaughn, Christopher and Kimberly, 44–45
Vause, John, 208
Vecsey, Laura, 94
View, The, 9–10, 11–13

Virgin Mary, 153–157, 158
voice-morphing technology, 15–16
Voight, Jon, 226
"Vote for the Worst" campaign, 122–123

W

Wachowski brothers, 224–225
Wag the Dog, 215, 217, 219–220
Wahlberg, Mark, 232
Waitley, Denis, 108
Wal-Mart, 127
"war" on Christmas, 165–175
War on Christmas, The (Gibson), 166, 172
Waterston, Sam, 234
We Can Remember It for You Wholesale (Dick), 221
weight loss, 111–112
Weir, Peter, 224
Wicker Man, The, 232–233
Will, George, 55
Williams, Montel, 109, 147
"willing audience" factor, 150–151
Wilson, Luke, 133
Winfrey, Oprah, 49, 105–107, 109, 114
Wolfe, Tom, 44
World Championship of Online Poker controversy, 64
World Series, 93, 94, 96
World Series of Poker, 59, 62–63, 182
World Trade Center attack, 3–4, 6–8, 9–17
World Trade Organization protests, 128
Wright, Howard C., 131

Y

Yankees, New York, 92–93, 95, 96, 208